E.52.00

MPLS

M P L S

IMPLEMENTING
THE TECHNOLOGY

Eric W. Gray

Addison-Wesley

Boston • San Francisco • New York • Toronto • Montreal
London • Munich • Paris • Madrid
Capetown • Sydney • Tokyo • Singapore • Mexico City

The publisher offers discounts on this book when ordered in quantity for special sales. For more information, please contact:

Pearson Education Corporate Sales Division
One Lake Street
Upper Saddle River, NJ 07458
(800) 382-3419
corpsales@pearsontechgroup.com

Visit AW on the Web: www.awl.com/cseng/

Library of Congress Cataloging-in-Publication Data
Gray, Eric W.
    MPLS : implementing the technology / Eric W. Gray
        p. cm.
    Includes bibliographical references and index.
    ISBN 0-201-65762-7
    1. MPLS standard. I. Title.

    TK5105.573 .G73 2001
    004.6'2--dc21

                                                                    00-067549

ISBN 0-201-65762-7
Text printed on recycled paper
1 2 3 4 5 6 7 8 9 10—CRS—0504030201
First printing, March 2001

To my father,

Lawrence Sherman Gray.

CONTENTS

Part I

AN OVERVIEW OF LABEL SWITCHING   1

Chapter 1   THE IDEA. **3**

Chapter 2   BRIEF HISTORY OF MPLS **21**

Part II

DETAILS OF THE STANDARD   105

Chapter 6   IMPLEMENTATION ALTERNATIVES. . 107

Chapter 7   SERVICES 147

LIST OF FIGURES

LIST OF TABLES

INTRODUCTION

Multiprotocol Label Switching (MPLS) is the industry-standard approach developed by the Internet Engineering Task Force (IETF)[1] for reducing the complexity of forwarding in a network. MPLS is many things to many people, but it is first and foremost an approach for achieving the simplified forwarding characteristics of layer 2 (link layer) switching technologies while retaining the equally desirable flexibility and scalability of layer 3 (network layer) routing. Using MPLS, a routing decision is made at one network device, allowing similar devices to forward data using a simplified label-switching paradigm. Because MPLS reduces the work of the network by reducing the number of times that a routing decision must be made, it offers improved solutions to many routing problems.

Currently, the two most important uses of MPLS are traffic engineering and virtual private networks (VPNs), in that order. Although both can and are performed currently using existing standard protocols, MPLS makes these tasks simpler because it is possible to take advantage of the separation of routing and forwarding to reduce or eliminate some of the limitations of routing.

In traffic engineering, for example, it is possible to specify explicit routes during the process of setting up a path so that data may be rerouted around network hot spots. Network hot spots (congestion points) develop because routing tends to converge on selection of a single least-cost path to each possible (aggregate) destination. Using an explicit route to direct significant portions of this traffic to parts of the network that are not selected by the routing process allows packets to bypass network trouble spots by (partially) ignoring routing.

---

1. The IETF is a community of scientists, engineers, and industry experts working to establish how networks and network components work together. The standardization process within the IETF is driven by "consensus and working code." For more about the IETF, see http://www.ietf.org/overview.

MPLS may also be used in a number of ways to provide for tunneling private network traffic across public or backbone infrastructure, as is often necessary in support of virtual private networks. Network operators can use MPLS to tunnel packets between VPN sites, making address translation and more costly tunneling approaches unnecessary.

MPLS is potentially useful for other applications as well. For example, MPLS is likely to be fully supported on Linux platforms used at small Internet service providers (ISPs), businesses, and residences to provide network access for multiple computers. Using MPLS to forward packets via a software router may make a noticeable difference in the performance of the host being used as a router, allowing the Linux station to be used, for example, for network management, administrative and accounting applications, and other purposes (such as playing Civilization or Pod Racer).

MPLS does not represent a merger of the link and network layers. Instead, it interacts with both layers in a role as the arbitrator of layer 2 and layer 3 technologies. MPLS defines an encapsulation that resides between the network-layer and link-layer encapsulations, but—in some cases—it also defines values for significant field positions in the link-layer encapsulation itself. This is the case for MPLS used with Asynchronous Transfer Mode (ATM) and Frame Relay, for example. The desirable features of link-layer behavior may be achieved by assigning values to fields in the link-layer encapsulation, using a shim-layer encapsulation residing between the link-layer and network-layer encapsulations, or embedding a fixed-length value within the network-layer encapsulation.[2] MPLS also includes definitions for mechanisms for establishing label values in link-layer and MPLS shim-layer fields and for using these values in processing packets. Packet processing and forwarding is, of course, the ultimate reason to use the technology.

MPLS is not expected to be an end-to-end solution. There is relatively little to gain from having host involvement in MPLS label allocation and use. In addition, MPLS scalability depends in part on limiting the scope of MPLS domains. Merging of labels becomes essential as the size of an MPLS domain increases, yet merging cannot extend all the way to end points—unless, for example, there is only one receiver for traffic in the Internet. Finally, use of labels in forwarding implies a strong trust relationship be-

---

2. This final option was an early proposal for use with Internet Protocol version 6.

tween systems allocating labels and systems using them. That level of trust relationship does not currently exist end to end in the Internet.

Basic MPLS concepts can be summarized as follows:

- MPLS uses fixed-length labels to represent arbitrary information about packets. This might be information normally included with the packet, or it might be information known about a stream of packets that would not normally be included with each packet.

- A label is used to locally identify data packets that require equivalent forwarding.

- The fixed-length-label representation of forwarding information simplifies decisions based on using an exact-match algorithm. This simplified forwarding paradigm is called *label switching*.

- A router that participates in label switching is a *label switching router* (LSR).

- Labels are added at an MPLS ingress point, swapped at intermediate LSRs, and removed at an MPLS egress point. The path along which this occurs for any particular starting label is called a *label-switched path* (LSP).

About This Book

This book is intended to be a self-contained reference for MPLS technology. However, MPLS as a technology interacts with a large number of other technologies, such as various routing protocols, link-layer technologies, and—in theory at least—network-layer technologies. This book does not describe the specifics of individual routing protocols except as they directly relate to MPLS. There are many good reference books on routing and network- and link-layer technologies.

This book provides an overview of the various technologies that led to the development of MPLS. A relatively high-level summary of the history of the development process is useful in understanding some of the choices made in that process. However, this book's goal is to make the protocol itself understandable, so the focus is on the protocol details that resulted from the process of merging the various proposals rather than on a detailed analysis and comparison of each proposal. Books that do a good job of comparing at least the early proposals already exist.

The material in this book is based on publicly available information. Statements made in this book can be verified by anyone wishing to do so. Of course, not all of the public information is consistent. In particular, for several topics that are completely unavoidable in a serious attempt to talk about label switching, it is not possible to distill a common conclusion from the available information—or, at least, it is not possible to do so objectively. Information presented by the various participants often contains obscure references to information that might or might not be well known (even if not publicly available) and is often starkly at odds with related information provided by others. An example of this problem is the continuing debate over which signaling protocol is most useful under what circumstances. Consequently, the goal of trying to make the MPLS technology easily understandable is slightly at odds with the goal of being fair and objective in discussing the results of the development of the technology standard. Too much fairness and objectivity would result in too much ambiguity. I hope I've done a reasonably good job of achieving the understandability goal without compromising too much on fairness and objectivity.

Who Should Read This Book

This book assumes that the reader has heard of the MPLS technology and is at least somewhat aware of the terminology. A glossary is provided to help fill in any gaps in the reader's MPLS-related vocabulary, and I've made every effort to make it possible for anyone to get a better understanding of the technology by reading this book.

You may be interested in this book because you are a network engineer, a network planner or architect, or other person thinking about deploying MPLS in your own network. You may find this book interesting if you are a technical manager or an engineer thinking of implementing the technology in your products. You might be a student who has volunteered your time and energy to study another tough subject. Or you may simply have heard of the technology and are interested in seeing where reading up on it might take you. It is possible that you might have picked this book off a shelf—either at a bookstore or in a technical library—without ever having heard of the technology, but it is not very likely. MPLS is, after all, yet another member of the new generation of four-letter acronyms ("ATM" having fairly demonstrated that the age of three-letter acronyms has passed) and will most likely not be of urgent interest to someone who has not even heard of it.

At the time that I was writing this book, there were no reasonably up-to-date detailed technical books on MPLS and yet there were a lot of questions and general interest in this exciting new technology. The fact that you've read this far indicates that you are one of the many people with questions about this new technology. Thus, unless you're still convinced that MPLS is the abbreviation for Minneapolis, the fact that you still have this book in front of you indicates that you are likely to be someone who should read it.

What You Need to Know Already

To make the most of this book, the reader should have a basic understanding of networking technologies such as routing, switching, data transport, encapsulation, signaling, and control functions and issues. This book contains numerous references to books on these basic topics. These references should be used for supplemental reading in the event that some basic concepts are not clear. If you are a network engineer or a technical manager, the material in this book—together with a basic understanding of data networking—should be sufficient for you to be able to make intelligent decisions about implementing and deploying the technology. If you are an implementer, this book should provide a solid grounding in the technology. However, before you will be able to do much with this knowledge, you will need to read the particular related texts that will provide you with more detail concerning the specifics of what you are trying to implement. This is especially true with respect to specific routing protocols, quality-of-service models (QoS), and virtual private networks.

How to Read This Book

The material in this book is organized in such a way that almost anyone can read it and obtain some benefit from doing so. For example, the first chapter provides an overview of the ideas embodied in the technology. For some people, the first chapter may be all that they need to read. As another example, I have used footnotes extensively. My hope in so doing is to make it possible for readers to simply ignore the footnotes if they are not interested in background discussions or in where a particular comment or observation originated. Using footnotes in this way allows many readers somewhat greater ease in following the flow of the ideas being discussed.

I have also tried to organize the chapters in such a way as to let each stand on its own in addressing a particular subset of MPLS functionality that might be of interest to people who are not as interested in other chapters. For example, readers who are not interested in the history of MPLS may skip Chapter 2 entirely with little loss in understanding of, say, the useful-ness of MPLS for a specific network application. Of course, there will be readers who are interested in all aspects of the technology. Therefore, I set out with the dual goals of making each chapter an integral whole and of providing cross-references to tie the material together for those who are interested in the whole picture.

The actual layout of the book is as follows. Part I, consisting of Chapters 1 to 5, provides an overview of the MPLS technology. Part II, consisting of Chapters 6 and 7, digs into the details of the MPLS standard.

Chapter 1 describes the basics of the technology, using examples and pro-viding an overview of the technical details. The main concepts discussed include what label switching and label swapping are, how they compare with routing, and what is required to signal labels.

Chapter 2 sets forth the evolutionary process by which these revolutionary concepts developed. This brief chronicle starts with a prehistory that touches on some of the problems people were trying to solve, some of the earlier proposals for dealing with these problems, and the ways in which the problems themselves were evolving. The chapter then discusses the major proposals that actually drove the industry to develop one standard solution. Finally, it provides a summary of how the standard reached its present status. Time lines and other charts throughout the chapter show how various efforts influenced each other.

Chapters 3, 4, and 5 take the reader a little closer to the technology and its relationship to the networking world. Chapter 3 explains how MPLS must interact with routing and with the network and link layers in order to provide forwarding services at least as good as those that currently exist. It also provides an overview of the benefits MPLS is expected to provide within this framework. Chapter 4 details MPLS system architecture, including components, functions, and operating modes. Chapter 5 explains where specific MPLS encapsulation and signaling approaches are most applicable. These chapters provide the groundwork for more detailed discussion in the remaining chapters.

Chapter 6 provides detailed comparisons of MPLS and alternative approaches to solving the same problems. It illustrates how MPLS differs from other approaches and what the benefits are in using MPLS. This chapter also shows how MPLS is supported over various technologies, including Asynchronous Transfer Mode (ATM), Frame Relay, Packet over SONET (POS), and Ethernet.

Finally, Chapter 7 describes how services such as QoS, traffic engineering, and virtual private networks may be supported using MPLS.

An extensive glossary provides both acronym expansions and definitions of terms and phrases used in this book.

ACKNOWLEDGMENTS

I wish to thank the following people for their careful reviews of this book during its development:

Jhilmil Kochar
Loa Andersson
Muckai K. Girish of SBC Technology Resources, Inc.
Radia Perlman
Randal T. Abler of the Georgia Institute of Technology
Rob Blais of the University of New Hampshire InterOperability Lab
Ron Bonica
Ross W. Callon
Thomas D. Nadeau of Cisco Systems, Inc.
Tom Herbert
Walt Wimmer of Marconi Communications

Their efforts did much to encourage me and help to improve the readability and accuracy of the work.

I also wish to thank coworkers who offered encouragement and support throughout the time I spent working on the book. I particularly want to thank Barbara Fox, Pramod Kalyanasundaram, and Vasanthi Thirumalai (then of Lucent Technologies) and people I worked with at Zaffire, including Fong Liaw, George Frank, John Yu, and Michael Yao.

Nobody helped quite as much as those closest to me. I offer a very special thanks to the members of my family who bore with me during the many crunch periods.

Finally, I wish to acknowledge the help and patience of the staff at Addison-Wesley, in particular: Karen Gettman, Mary Hart, Emily Frey, and Marcy Barnes.

Part I

AN OVERVIEW OF LABEL SWITCHING

1

THE IDEA

*Anything that two consenting routers
do over a link layer is their own business.*
•Tony Li, ION mailing list, 8 November 1996

1.1 Label Switching

Switching data packets on the Internet can be compared to an automated railway system in which a code is transmitted (or displayed) by the lead car. At every railway switching station, a switching system automatically cross-connects the track on which the cars are arriving with the track on which they are supposed to depart, based simply on the code used by the lead car. The cross-connect is maintained (one hopes) until the last car leaves the switching station, at which time the switching system is free to realign cross-connects for the next set of railway cars.

Of course, the lead car may use an arbitrarily complex code. The code may include where each car came from, where it is going, what it contains, and how it is to be routed at each switching station. It may also describe who owns each item contained in the car and whether or not those items have been inspected, have cleared customs, or are insured. You get the idea.

Much of this information may be needed if each switching station has to make an independent routing decision. For example, if there are goods on board that have not cleared customs or otherwise been inspected, it is possible that some switching stations may be required to divert the railway

3

cars to a location where this can take place. However, for more mundane railway cars and at many switching stations, the routing options are not so complicated and it is likely that many similar trains can be grouped into a class in which all class members are switched in the same way. In fact, such a switching system can realize substantial savings in storage if it stores exactly that information about each class that it needs to identify members of that class. The system then determines class membership by examining the code provided by the lead car and searching for a "best fit" among the routing information it has stored.

To understand why this may be important, imagine that the automated switching system supports well over a hundred million (10^8) railway terminal stations. Storing routing information based solely on source and destination would therefore require over 10^{16} route entries.[1] Additional information that might be required to identify an individual route would further compound this complexity.

However, performing a best-fit (or *longest-match,* in routing parlance) search at every switching station and for every set of railway cars has its own costs. The code used by the lead car must be successively compared with code fragments (following a decision tree), looking for the first point at which it does not match a code fragment on any subbranch of the decision tree. In practical usage, multiple comparisons are required in every case.

To put this cost in perspective, imagine that we're thinking of upgrading the automated switching system such that it can switch 20 million cars a second[2] and that we don't want to have cars sidetracked for an appreciable amount of time at every station. In this case, we would want to reduce the time it takes to match the code for the lead car with a routing entry by as much as possible. One way to do that would be to replace the complex code we've been using with a shorter one that exactly matches a code associated with an individual route entry at each switching station. This is, in essence, what Multiprotocol Label Switching (MPLS) does.

---

1. Numbers like this do not typically mean much to most people. If you could store a million route entries on a single grain of sand, and a million grains of sand weighed in at 1 pound, it would require 5 tons of sand to store this many route entries. That's a lot of silica.

2. For those readers with a solid grounding in physics, please ignore physical limitations in this analogy, such as those relating to friction, momentum, and the speed of light.

Let's examine this analogy and see how it equates to the general concept of routing and switching data packets. In the analogy, switching stations are equivalent to routers and switches, trains are equivalent to data packets, and tracks are equivalent to links and interfaces. Forwarding data packets is typically based on information contained in a header. This information is comparable to the code displayed by a lead car. The information contained in an Internal Protocol (IP) header, for example, can be fairly (if not quite arbitrarily) complex if IP options are used. In addition, network equipment (for example, firewalls) may be set up to inspect the contents of IP packets. Finally, the header may identify that a particular packet is to be handled in a different way (provided with special queuing or other treatment).

Most network-layer data packets are pretty mundane, however, and are routed based on a network-layer destination address at most network devices. This is a good thing because there are something like 100 million IP end stations in the Internet, and thus there is a need to be able to group destination addresses into classes.[3]

Aggregating route information using destination-based routing produces forwarding classes based on a network-layer address prefix. Because not all prefixes are the same length, routing decisions are typically based on a longest-match (best-fit) algorithm. The need to perform multiple comparisons establishes the maximum speed at which routing decisions can be made and thus sets the maximum rate at which a given routing device can forward packets for any particular device's processing speed.

The maximum speed at which one can forward packets determines the efficiency of the utilization of a particular line speed. For example, if the interface line speed is roughly 2.5 gigabits per second (corresponding to OC-48 SONET)[4] and the packet size distribution is 64/200/1500 (minimum/average/maximum) bytes per packet, one can compute the approximate required packet-processing speed (for approximately 100% utilization) as follows:

---

3. It is important to distinguish the concept of grouping destination addresses into classes based on routing protocol interactions and route aggregation from the concept of class-full IP addressing (based on class A, B, and C IP network prefixes, for example).

4. Synchronous Optical Network (SONET) provides the physical layer for many layer 2 (L2) technologies, including Asynchronous Transfer Mode (ATM) and Packet over SONET (POS). See Siller and Shafi (1996) for more information.

$$S_{max} = (2.5 \times 10^9)/(64 \times 8) \cong 5 \text{ million packets/second}$$
$$S_{avg} = (2.5 \times 10^9)/(200 \times 8) \cong 1.5 \text{ million packets/second}$$
$$S_{min} = (2.5 \times 10^9)/(1500 \times 8) \cong 200 \text{ thousand packets/second}$$

If we now want to introduce 10-Gbps line rates (corresponding to OC-192) into this network, we need to be able to increase the packet-processing rate to roughly 20 million packets per second (in order to handle a continuous stream of minimal-size packets).

To distinguish between forwarding based on the longest match and forwarding based on an exact match, many people refer to the former as *routing* and the latter as *switching*. This key distinction is used in this book.

Bridging, Switching, and Label Switching

Because bridging technologies necessarily perform forwarding based on an exact match (link-layer addressing is usually not based on locality and cannot be aggregated in any useful way), bridging is often equated with switching. This comparison is useful to many people who are familiar with the differences in complexity in bridging and routing because it can help them to understand the advantages that switching has to offer in comparison with routing.

In addition, there are technologies that have always been referred to as switching—for example, circuit switching, ATM, and Frame Relay. People familiar with these switching technologies generally associate switching with the idea of higher forwarding speeds. The higher forwarding speeds these technologies offer are, at least in part, due to the simplified forwarding made possible by using an exact match on a fixed-length field. Unlike bridging and some other switching technologies, however, ATM and Frame Relay may exchange the values on which forwarding is based. For example, a Frame Relay Data Link Connection Identifier (DLCI) is used in conjunction with an input interface to determine both the output interface and the new DLCI.[5]

---

5. Frame Relay switches may use either or both of two different DLCI values—10 and 23 bits—depending on values assigned in other bit positions in the Frame Relay header. This is not precisely a fixed-length field, but it can be treated as one by assuming that a device does the lookup in two stages: determining size and looking up value.

If a network device is able consistently to make forwarding decisions based on well-known bit positions in message headers, the process of making the decision is very simple. This is true regardless of the header to which this applies (whether it is a layer 2, layer 3, or higher-layer header). Values in these bit positions may be used as a control word that sets up a temporary channel from the interface on which the packet was received to the interface on which the packet is to be retransmitted, thus switching the packet. (This is intended as an illustrative example; many implementations use different approaches.) A common approach is the use of content addressable memory: The significant header data is used to access a data record in high-speed memory that is then used to switch the data to the appropriate output interface. The data record may also include replacement header information. Switching is based on the ability to consistently determine how to forward packets by examining well-known bit positions in message headers.

Forwarding Complexity

Prior to the introduction of MPLS (and related proposals), the forwarding decision was a great deal more complicated for routing than it was for any switching technology. From the earliest generations, routers have been tasked with dealing with multiple paths across a network and, over time, multiple network layers and corresponding packet formats.[6] Routing is also required to provide access to the global Internet—that is, to act as a gateway between a private network (intranet) and any and all other networks (extranets), including the Internet. The Internet is orders of magnitude larger and more complicated than any currently existing bridged network segment.

Of course, there is a direct relationship between the complexity of any task and the cost of acquiring and maintaining the equipment necessary for performing the task:

$$\text{Cost}_{\text{acquire}} + \text{Cost}_{\text{maintain}} \cong K \times \text{Complexity}$$

---

6. The network layer is layer 3 in the Open Systems Interconnection (OSI) reference model; examples include Internet Protocol version 4 (IPv4) and Internetwork Packet Exchange (IPX). This book assumes the reader is reasonably familiar with at least the lower layers of the OSI reference model. See Black (1991) for a detailed discussion of this reference model.

From this equation, we can make an inference about the relative costs of bridging (or switching) and analogous routing functions. If the complexity of a routing function is orders of magnitude greater than the complexity of a bridging function, then the cost of the routing function (in terms of initial outlay and continuing operating costs) should be orders of magnitude greater than the cost of an analogous bridging function. That this assumption is not always reflected in equipment prices is attributable to at least some of the following factors:

- Equipment manufacturers use proprietary techniques to eliminate as much of the additional complexity as possible.
- The cost of routing, bridging, and switching functions is only a part of the total cost of the devices used to provide these functions.
- Part of the initial outlay may be hidden in indirect expenses relating to the cost of maintenance agreements, service contracts, and upgrades.

The remainder of this section provides detailed reasons why routing is generally more complex than either switching or bridging.

MULTIPLE PATHS

Supporting multiple paths and a larger and more complicated network structure makes support for frequent changes in topology with minimal packet loss a critical feature of routing protocols and devices. Because of the sheer size of the Internet, for example, an indispensable characteristic of any routing mechanism is the ability to continue to forward data during a network transition. Some part of the Internet is bound to be in a state of change at just about any point in time. Hence, routers and routing protocols have evolved—and continue to evolve—mechanisms for continuing to forward data. Most such mechanisms are based on using distributed route computation. At any given instance in time, a router is likely to believe it knows the right thing to do with a packet (thus avoiding dropping it as much as possible). However, the "right thing to do" (as determined using route table information) is subject to change and is a result of information that may not be in synchronization with that being used by other network devices making similar forwarding decisions for the same packets in the same network.

Because of the size of the Internet, it is also necessary to have multiple paths between any sets of end points. Topological size (that is, the number of devices and links that are required to be working to maintain connectivity between end points) dictates a need for decreased reliance on any single link or device. Geographical size, however, makes it highly desirable to avoid underutilizing any existing links. Thus, routing data packets needs to be done by devices able to deal with multiple active paths.

Because it is possible that the information used to make forwarding decisions is not consistent at all routers in any portion of the network, data packets can take the wrong path and even loop. Some part of the forwarding decision process must be to determine if data is looping too much (consuming too many network resources). This typically is done on a packet-by-packet basis (using Time to Live [TTL], for example). Routing technologies consequently rely on loop mitigation approaches. Use of TTL, for example, prevents packets from consuming more than a fixed amount of network resources (on a per-packet basis).

Switching technologies construct a simplified network topology that restricts the paths available for forwarding, thus making looping impossible. Prior to constructing (or restricting) forwarding paths, switching technologies typically do not forward data packets. Consequently, a transient in a switched network will usually result in a total loss of use of the network until the new topology is completely determined.

Bridging technologies, for example, use the spanning tree algorithm to construct a connected, loop-free forwarding tree.[7] This is accomplished by disabling forwarding using certain interfaces at each bridge. Looping data is thus avoided by choosing not to use some network resources.

Other switching technologies use a connection-oriented approach based on virtual circuits that are similarly loop free. Consequently, switches do not have to check to see if packets are looping because packets follow a path that has been determined to be loop free during the setup process. Use of virtual circuits does not necessarily guarantee equal use of network resources, however, and it is disruptive to move a virtual circuit from one path to another in an attempt to redistribute traffic.

---

7. See Section 3.3 of Perlman (1992) for more on the spanning tree algorithm.

Routers generally attempt to detect that a loop exists during the process of forwarding data, whereas switches generally attempt to eliminate loops prior to forwarding data.

MULTIPLE NETWORK LAYERS

Support for multiple network layers complicates the process of determining significant fields (or bit positions) in packet headers. The need to first determine what network layer is used in each packet further complicates the process of performing a longest-match comparison with values in the packet header. Each additional network layer supported by any routing device introduces a new branch in processing the packets being forwarded by the device. Branching processes are especially difficult to optimize.

Until very recently, routers in enterprise (private) networks were required to support several network-layer (or higher) protocols. In particular, IPv4, IPX, and AppleTalk were in use in many corporate networks. Recent trends have been toward exclusive use of IPv4. Ideally, all networks would eventually switch to exclusive use of IPv4; however, Internet Protocol version 6 (IPv6) is looming on the horizon.

One solution used in the past relied on a simplistic optimization approach: Optimize for the dominant (or normal) case only. This meant that forwarding of IPv4 packets with no IP options in use would be optimized, whereas forwarding of other network-layer packets or of IP packets with options specified might be performed in a substantially suboptimal way. Because of the possibility of a transition in the network layer from IPv4 to IPv6 at some point in the future, it is very likely that many routers will need to support both versions of the Internet Protocol. Consequently, router manufacturers are less willing to assume that it is sufficient to optimize packet processing for only one network-layer protocol.

An efficient switching solution to the problem of having a variety of network-layer protocols is to perform a forwarding decision on the basis of information that is not dependent on the network layer—at least on a per-packet basis. For instance, switches that use virtual circuits can establish virtual circuits for the purpose of switching specific sets of network-layer packets along a path. If the path is determined during virtual circuit setup, using the same route determination process that would otherwise be applied on a per-packet basis, then these switches need only optimize the process of forwarding along the virtual circuit. The actual forwarding process is thus independent of the network layer used in making a route determination.

Routers decide how to forward each packet by determining the route for the packet from the L3 (network layer) header and the router's route table. Switches decide how to forward each packet using a function that is separate from the process of determining the route for packets having any particular L3 header.

INTERNET ACCESS

Access to the Internet's resources requires using an addressing structure that allows aggregation based on location. Otherwise, every routing device would need to store routing information for more than 100 million distinct addresses.[8] The network layer provides this addressing structure. Network-layer addresses consist of network addresses (or network numbers) and host addresses. In addition, host addresses are typically grouped into sub-networks (subnets). Having this sort of hierarchical grouping of addresses greatly simplifies the requirements for route storage in routing devices. It also complicates the process of making a routing decision by introducing a need to match packet header information to route entries using a longest-match algorithm. In addition, routers frequently serve as gateways between network domains—imposing filtering, security, and other complicating factors on the already complex routing task.[9] The gateway function is an essential part of access to the Internet.

The additional complexity associated with domain boundaries has an impact on both the process of forwarding data and the process of comput-

---

8. IPv4 addresses are 32 bits long, allowing for a maximum of over 4 billion addresses. Many of these addresses are reserved or otherwise not useful in typical routing across the Internet. IPX—which is gradually being phased out—and IPv6 both offer larger address spaces. At the time of this writing, it is generally accepted that there are in the neighborhood of 100 million active IP end stations at peak activity moments on the Internet.

9. It is not the intent of this book to become bogged down in a general discussion of routing issues, technologies, and complexities, except as required for understanding engineering decisions made in label-switching design. See Chapters 9 to 11 of Perlman (1992), Chapter 5 of Tanenbaum (1996), or Chapters 12 and 13 of Moy (1998) for more detailed discussions of these topics.

ing routes. Data forwarding is affected because filtering, address translation, or header manipulation impose requirements to look more closely at the packets being forwarded. The process of computing routes is affected because the information shared across domain boundaries by routing protocols may be constrained by policy considerations or limitations in the ability to import routes, which may lead to inaccurate data.

The net effect of these two complicating factors is that it is possible for the policies affecting forwarding and route computation to be inconsistent. This increases the likelihood of incorrectly forwarding data packets—leading to packet loss and, potentially, to lost network connectivity.

A New Switching Paradigm

Switching technologies such as Frame Relay and Asynchronous Transfer Mode (ATM) significantly reduced the distinction between bridging and routing. ATM, for example, uses routing for virtual circuit (VC) setup and switching of actual data packets. These switching technologies represented the first industry-wide attempt to uniformly separate route determination from forwarding in data networks.[10]

The general approach, suggested by the ATM-specific paradigm, is to use routing protocol exchanges, router configuration information, and routing decisions to set up virtual connections for streams of data. In the MPLS analogue, a virtual connection for a specific data stream is established across some subset of network devices based on the routing decisions these devices would make for the actual data in those streams. Labels corresponding to ATM virtual path and virtual channel identifiers (VPI/VCI or VPCI) locally identify the virtual connection. Once a virtual connection is established, the data packets may be forwarded based on the labels assigned, allowing for a high-speed forwarding implementation similar to ATM.

Unlike ATM, however, the label-switching approach is generally applicable to a number of network technologies,[11] does not always require fragmen-

---

10. Note that many switching solutions in the past were characterized by separation of route determination and forwarding, including Public Switched Telephone Networks (PSTN).

11. For example, definitions for label switching over PPP, Ethernet, ATM, and Frame Relay are currently relatively mature.

tation of data packets into cells, and allows direct use of native routing information and technology. Label switching is the process of making a simplified forwarding decision based on a fixed-length label; this label can be included in a Frame Relay DLCI, an ATM VPI/VCI, or at the head of an MPLS shim header in other technologies.

1.2 Label Swapping

Not all switching technologies modify the value used in making a forwarding decision. Circuit switching (for example, in voice telephony) and transparent bridging (in data networking) are instances that do not modify the value used to decide how to forward information. The trouble with approaches like these is that the values used have to be established as unique for all members of a network using this common technology. In other words, the labels used are more than locally significant.

Label switching relies on label swapping to preserve the local significance of a label. In addition to enabling the switching function, the label in a label-encapsulated data packet received on an input interface is used to determine the label that will be used in transmitting the altered data packet on an output interface. This is highly analogous to VPI/VCI switching in ATM, for example, in which the input interface and VPI/VCI determine the output interface and VPI/VCI. Local significance is important in reducing the complexity of the process of negotiating labels because it is only necessary to know that the label is locally unique, and the label does not have any nonlocal meaning.

In addition to possibly swapping the input label with an output label, one or more labels may be popped from the label stack of the received data packet, and one or more labels may be pushed onto the label stack for the packet to be transmitted.[12] In fact, label swapping itself may be logically generalized as the degenerate case of a pop (one or more labels) and push (one or more labels) in which exactly one label is popped and exactly one pushed. (Most implementations would probably not use this approach for practical reasons. The pop-push operation is more complicated than simply

---

12. The concept of the label stack is discussed in detail in the section MPLS System Components in Chapter 4.

overwriting the label field.) Pushing and popping of labels (adding or removing one or more labels) is discussed in greater detail in the Label Stack Manipulation section in Chapter 4.

Label swapping effectively establishes the label switching router (also known as a label switch router or LSR) as a media end point, defining the local scope of the label being swapped and, thus, the domain within which the label is significant and must be unique. This limitation on the scope of a label greatly increases the scalability of label switching because any label need only be unique between the LSR that allocates it and the LSR that prepends it to a packet.

1.3 Signaling Labels

The significance of a label received at an input interface is that it is used to

- Determine what output interface, if any, will be used in forwarding data
- Determine what label operations (push, pop, swap) are to be performed
- Determine what label is to be used on transmission at the output interface

All of the LSRs within the domain of significance of a particular label must agree on what that significance is if the data packets encapsulated with that label are to be correctly forwarded. For example, in Figure 1.1, if a data stream is intended to flow from LSR 1 to LSR 2 and be further forwarded by LSR 2, then LSR 2 must know how to interpret the label used by LSR 1 for this data stream. In addition, for media where other LSRs may also see packets in this stream (LSR 3 in Figure 1.1), those LSRs must be able to determine whether it is appropriate for them to forward these packets as well.

Although the significance of a label might be established via configuration (or provisioning), this will prove to be an onerous task if large numbers of label-switched paths (LSPs) are required. In addition, this method will not allow for the dynamic changes in routes currently supported in routed networks. Finally, as the amount of configuration increases, the probability of configuration error approaches certainty.

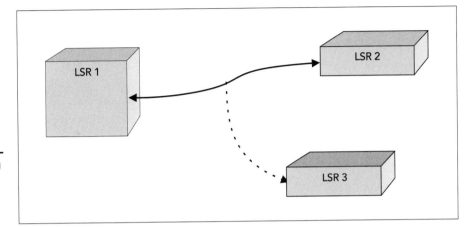

FIGURE 1.1

Label switching routers with multipoint-to-multipoint connectivity

Consequently, label switching requires mechanisms for signaling, or distributing, labels within a domain of label significance.[13] In general, LSRs that share knowledge of the significance of a set of labels are adjacent—at least within the context of the signaling mechanisms used to distribute those labels (Figure 1.2). (Examples of mechanisms for distributing labels are discussed in Label Distribution in Chapter 6.) These mechanisms must ensure that label significance is consistent both among various adjacent LSRs and with respect to each label's meaning at each LSR.

Consistency relative to a label's meaning is slightly different from simply keeping each adjacent LSR consistent concerning label and forwarding information. The information used by the routing function at each LSR is subject to constant change—not only in terms of how a particular stream of data is forwarded, but also in terms of whether a particular message is part of that stream. Thus it is necessary for adjacent LSRs to be able to negotiate more or fewer labels as needed to support changing forwarding requirements. An example of this is when routes are aggregated and the aggregate is associated with a single label. If a subset of the routes thus aggregated subsequently changes (such that the subset diverges from the remaining routes associated with the aggregate label), the LSRs will need to negotiate one or more new labels.

---

13. Labels are usually significant only for a single peer-to-peer link. The term *domain of label significance* is used here to include cases in which it is possible that more than a single link is involved—as may be the case with as-yet-to-be-defined multicast label switching, for example.

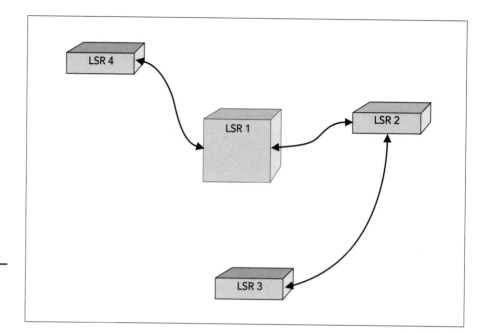

FIGURE 1.2

Adjacency
among label
switching
routers

The simplest way to ensure that any label is consistent among adjacent LSRs and consistent with its meaning relative to specific forwarding is to piggyback the labels being distributed using the same messages that the routing function at each LSR uses to establish forwarding. In order to piggyback labels, however, it is necessary for forwarding information to be shared between routers via protocols that meet the following conditions:

- The protocol consists of message exchanges between adjacent protocol peers.
- There is an exact mapping between effectively adjacent peers with respect to the protocol itself and adjacent LSRs within the label-switching context among all adjacent LSRs.

It is also useful if the protocol itself supports mechanisms for transporting labels appropriate to a specific forwarding medium.

To illustrate the first condition, imagine a protocol consisting of message exchanges between LSRs that may or may not be adjacent. Labels attached to such messages will not be useful in cases where the LSRs are not adjacent because the label negotiated in this way will need to be interpreted or assigned by devices not participating in the negotiation.

Note that the adjacency here is in terms of how the labeled messages are transported from one LSR to another. If the labeled packets are L2 encapsulated, the presence of one or more transparent bridges between two LSRs does not affect their adjacency. In the same way, an LSP may be used to provide adjacency (via label stacking, as discussed elsewhere in this book), as may any of several other tunneling approaches that allow transparent packet transport.[14]

In Figure 1.2, if LSRs 2, 3, and 4 are using protocol XYZ and LSR 1 is not, protocol XYZ cannot be used to piggyback labels between LSRs 2 and 4 unless a more direct adjacency is established between these two devices.

Similarly, there must be a contextual mapping between the logically adjacent peers in both the piggyback protocol candidate and MPLS contexts. If routers are adjacent with respect to a piggyback candidate protocol but not adjacent with respect to MPLS, the labels that might be piggybacked on the candidate protocol would be meaningless in the MPLS context because intervening LSRs would be unable to interpret (and properly forward packets using) these labels. In the same way, adjacent LSRs can only piggyback label distribution on protocols in which all adjacent LSRs participate and are logically adjacent.[15] Otherwise, some of the adjacent LSRs would not be aware of the labels being distributed.

Let's use Border Gateway Protocol (BGP) as an example to illustrate this concept. Labels may be negotiated using BGP messages to piggyback label assignments from one BGP peer to another (see Piggyback Label Distribution Using BGP in Chapter 6). For these labels to be useful, however, the peers participating in the negotiation must be either physically adjacent or must be logically adjacent via an LSP between them. If they are

---

14. In general, tunneling approaches that treat the encapsulated contents of the packet as opaque—that is, the approach does not differentiate forwarding based on anything beyond the encapsulation provided in the tunneling approach and does not alter the contents of encapsulated packets—can be used to provide transparent packet transport. This book discusses tunneling only briefly (see Chapter 6) and then mostly as it relates to label switching.

15. Again, an understanding of transparency is assumed. Border Gateway Protocol (BGP) extensions are defined for piggybacking MPLS labels on BGP exchanges in such a way that route reflectors are transparent (since they are not part of the forwarding path) in the labeling context. See Bates and Chandrasekeran (1996) for more information on BGP reflectors, and Rekhter and Rosen (2000) for details of how this is accomplished.

not directly adjacent and there is not a continuous LSP between them, any labels negotiated between them will have no meaning at some point between the two peers. In this example, two adjacent BGP speakers are not logically adjacent LSRs.

The protocol being considered as a candidate for piggyback distribution of MPLS labels should have defined mechanisms or protocol extensions to allow the labels to be transported via intervening devices in the event that protocol peers are not physically adjacent. It would not do, for instance, if the messages carrying MPLS labels were being discarded as incompatible with the base protocol in intermediate systems.

Protocol extensions used to carry labels must be defined for carrying the appropriate type of label as well. For example, a candidate piggyback protocol needs to be able to include an ATM VPI/VCI in order to establish LSPs for use with ATM links.

Under circumstances in which no acceptable candidate protocol for piggyback distribution exists, labels must be distributed using a protocol specifically provided for that purpose. A specific label distribution protocol is also needed to permit negotiation of label parameters and provide acknowledgment or negative acknowledgment (ACK/NAK) responses to label assignments when piggyback protocols do not themselves provide mechanisms for doing these things.[16]

MPLS provides the ability to make one routing decision and a series of switching decisions along an LSP.

The automated railway system introduced at the start of this chapter presented an analogy of the routing problem. Imagine that each switching station is able to tell all of its neighbors exactly what to put on the lead car of each train. It makes sense, in this case, for the switching station to decide exactly how many different ways it might want to switch any trains it receives from any particular neighboring switching station and then give that neighbor a set of labels to attach to each train. It also makes sense for

---

16. A label may need to be refused, for example, if it is not within the capabilities of the local LSR to use that label. This can prove to be difficult to do if the protocol does not provide reciprocal messaging or if there is no reverse traffic for a significant period of time and no Null message is defined for the protocol (i.e., a message that—although it contains nothing specific to the protocol—will not be discarded without further processing by an intermediate system).

a local switching station to select labels that do not require a complex matching algorithm in order to simplify the decision-making process regarding forwarding as much as possible. In the simplest case, this is what MPLS allows routers to do, via signaling.

References

Bates, Tony, and Ravishanker Chandrasekeran. 1996 (June). BGP route reflection: An alternative to full mesh IBGP. RFC 1966. Available at http://www.isi.edu/in-notes/rfc1966.txt.

Black, Uyless. 1991. *OSI: A Model for Computer Communications Standards.* Englewood Cliffs, NJ: Prentice Hall, 1991.

Moy, John T. 1998. *OSPF: Anatomy of an Internet Routing Protocol.* Reading, MA: Addison-Wesley.

MPLS Internet Drafts. Available at http://ietf.cnri.reston.va.us/ids.by.wg/mpls.html.

Perlman, Radia. 1992. *Interconnections: Bridges and Routers.* Reading, MA: Addison-Wesley.

Rekhter, Yakov, and Eric C. Rosen. Carrying label information in BGP-4; a work in progress.

Siller, Curtis A., and Mansoor Shafi, eds. 1996. *SONET/SDH: A Sourcebook of Synchronous Networking.* New York: IEEE Press.

Tanenbaum, Andrew S. 1996. *Computer Networks,* 3rd ed. Upper Saddle River, NJ: Prentice Hall.

2

BRIEF HISTORY OF MPLS

In the real world, outcomes don't just happen.
They build up gradually as small chance events
become magnified by positive feedbacks.
•*Dr. Brian Arthur, quoted in* Complexity
(Waldrop 1992)

A thorough discussion of a technology is not truly complete without at least a summary of the history that went into making it. However, this chapter is essentially parenthetical. If you are not interested in the history of MPLS and how it developed out of a miasma of related technologies, skipping this chapter entirely will not prevent you from understanding the remaining chapters of this book.

2.1 Early Notions

 In retrospect, there were disconnects in the process of defining both switched virtual circuits (SVCs) and traffic management in ATM and the possibility of using these services in IP. These disconnects are not hard to understand for those people who were involved in the process. They occurred largely because of changes in market and product development directions stemming from the chaotic influence of market feedback. Similar feedback processes were involved in the standardization process as well. Where things ended up is not where things looked like they were heading at various stages in the process.

21

LAN Emulation

For example, LAN emulation (LANE) (ATM Forum 1997a) was developed because of a then-widespread belief that ATM to the desktop was the future direction of technology. LANE defined a client/server architecture and service implementation to support use of ATM switches in a bridged network. LANE focused on interworking with the dominant L2 technologies—specifically, IEEE standards 802.5 (Token Ring) and 802.3 (nearly identical to, and usually thought to include, Ethernet)—in order to support L2 technologies generally.[1] Work on developing LANE was coordinated with continuing efforts in the IEEE through the occasionally heroic efforts of people participating in multiple efforts.[2]

Multi-Protocol over ATM

Multi-protocol over ATM (MPOA) (ATM Forum 1997b) was developed in turn as an effort to extend the thinking (if not at all times the technology) used in developing LANE to be useful in a routed ATM network. MPOA also defines a client/server architecture and service implementation; however, MPOA applies to routing in all-ATM networks. MPOA focused on use of the Next Hop Resolution Protocol (NHRP), then being defined in the IETF working group Routing Over Large Clouds (ROLC). NHRP was intended to solve some of the problems then known to exist with Classical IP and ARP over ATM (CLIP) and for this reason was regarded by some to be the next-generation version of CLIP.[3] Work in developing MPOA was coordinated with ongoing efforts in the IETF in the same way that coordination occurred in LANE.[4]

---

1. The process of translating to and from other L2 standard technologies to either 802.5 or 802.3 is well understood in the industry. Thus, supporting either of these technologies would have been sufficient to support all standard L2 technologies.

2. Notably Norm Finn of Cisco Systems and Floyd Backes of 3Com Corporation, although others were involved as well.

3. NHRP specifically addresses issues regarding the logical mismatch between the ATM network and the IP overlay created using CLIP. Because this section is intended to provide a relatively brief historical perspective, the details of the specific problems are omitted.

4. George Swallow, Keith McCloghrie, and Yakov Rekhter (Cisco Systems), Joel Halpern (Newbridge Networks), and James Luciani (Bay Networks), as well as some others, participated in this coordination effort. George Swallow and Keith McCloghrie were the chairs

Although MPOA represented a major attempt to reconcile differences between what had developed as two separate routing models, one for ATM and one for IP,[5] its proponents were not at all in agreement about what the target model should be. Many people thought that the NHRP architecture offered a well-understood way to separate the route determination and forwarding functions, but the effort within the MPOA was split on how best to take advantage of this. Part of the effort centered on use of NHRP's client/server architecture to develop a virtual router architecture,[6] whereas another part of the effort centered on trying to define extensions to NHRP specific to ATM that would allow ATM-native traffic management features to be used in forwarding IP packets.

AVOIDING ROUTING OVERHEAD

To take direct advantage of ATM traffic management capabilities, it is necessary to avoid having the routing function involved in packet forwarding at every ATM switch router. CLIP allowed for this within a logical IP subnet (LIS) through the use of an IP-to-ATM address resolution protocol. However, a LIS has to be bounded on all sides by IP routers, and—in the absence of some other mechanism—packets are forwarded at the intervening routers by examining them at the IP layer and making a routing decision. In the absence of a mechanism that would make route determination unnecessary on a per-packet basis, it is difficult to provide end-to-end service assurances because the service is, in effect, interrupted by the routing process at each routing hop. NHRP was intended to provide such a mechanism by allowing an ingress point to an NBMA cloud to determine the

---

of the MPOA and LANE working groups, respectively. George Swallow later went on to become a co-chair of the ION working group and subsequently a co-chair of the MPLS working group. ION resulted from combining ROLC with the IP over ATM (IP-ATM) group. ION is a compound acronym meaning Internetworking over NBMA, where NBMA is an acronym for nonbroadcast multiple access media).

5. No discussion of this attempt to force the disparate technological efforts to converge would be complete without at least mentioning that there were many other proposals. Notable among these are RFC 1483 (Heinanen 1993), RFC 1755 (Perez et al. 1995), CLIP, I-PNNI, and PAR.

6. *Virtual routing,* in this context, is the separation of the routing and forwarding functions into different devices at potentially different physical locations.

NBMA-specific address of the appropriate egress from that cloud, thus allowing it to establish an SVC to that egress. MPOA uses NHRP to resolve egress ATM addresses in an ATM cloud.

Of course, if the routing overhead in any particular implementation is negligible, this aspect of the use of NHRP (and, consequently, MPOA) is not as important. However, implementations in which this was the case tended to be regarded as either largely theoretical or prohibitively expensive at the time these considerations were being made.

VIRTUAL ROUTING

Proponents of virtual routing architectures saw NHRP as a means to correct mismatches in physical ATM (or Frame Relay) connectivity and the routing topology. Specifically of concern were instances in which the mismatch could result in creating an SVC from an end station, or router, through some number of ATM switches to a router and from that router through one or more of the same ATM switches to an end station or another router. Constructing such an SVC would consume switch resources in both directions and—where the switch resources consumed include some level of queuing resources—could result in denial of services that the ATM infrastructure should be able to support. NHRP could be used to resolve an appropriate ATM address when this occurs, thus preventing the unnecessary double-booking of switch resources and allowing for more efficient use of the ATM infrastructure.

The value of this approach is sensitive to the number of ATM switches that are not also routers. Obviously, if every ATM switch is a router, then there will be no mismatch between ATM physical connectivity and the routing topology. If only one of every ten ATM switches is also a router, then some degree of topological mismatch may be unavoidable. At the time these issues were being considered, it was generally accepted that adding routing function to every ATM switch would be expensive, especially if one was trying to avoid the routing overhead at the same time.

NHRP ISSUES

An issue with the use of CLIP was that the size of a practical LIS was limited. All of the ATM end stations within a LIS would have to either maintain a large number of ATM connections to each other or open and close connections on a regular basis. Because each such end station within any one LIS would need to be connected to all others, the number of connections would be on the order of the square of the number of end stations that were participating in the LIS. Of course, opening and closing connections could be used to reduce the number of connections required, but this would increase the latency associated with establishing connections when they become needed and do not already exist. In the specific case in which a large number of routers are interconnected via a single LIS, this option would not be practical because there would be a high probability of constant traffic between any two routers in this configuration.

NHRP by itself does nothing to address this problem. Unless the protocol's usage is restricted in some way, NHRP cannot provide connectivity between ATM end stations in a cloud larger than was the case with a LIS in CLIP. Thus NHRP (and MPOA) is effective only when it is used to establish connectivity to a restricted subset of all end stations in any one ATM cloud. Such a restriction could be based on whether or not the connection was associated with some level of service assurance, whether or not there was a topological mismatch associated with the normally routed path, or both.[7]

Neither the ROLC group (and its successor, ION) nor the MPOA working group embarked on an effort to define signaling mechanisms and mappings between either Integrated Services or Differentiated Services such as quality of service (QoS) and ATM signaling parameters. This effort was the responsibility of the corresponding work groups within the IETF. Although a lot has been done in this area recently, the lack of progress at the time that NHRP was approaching becoming a Proposed Standard in the IETF made it hard for implementers to provide for inclusion of QoS parameters in NHRP messages.

Another issue with CLIP was the delay caused by the need to perform address resolution in order to determine the address of the ATM local destination for any particular IP destination address. This issue also exists

---

7. It turns out not to be very difficult to restrict extra-LIS connectivity in either of these ways. The Next Hop Server (NHS) can easily be implemented to classify NHRP requests based on the type of services requested. It can also be constructed in such a way as to pay attention to the ATM switch nodes in the path from the requester and to the corresponding next NHS (if any) or egress node.

when using NHRP—and is potentially worse because resolution requests may be forwarded multiple hops before an appropriate address resolution response can be returned. Implementations that attempt to compensate for this factor by "learning" ATM address associations would interfere with the efficacy of those implementations trying to restrict ATM connectivity.

Cell Switching Router

The routing decision on a per-packet basis can be avoided (in ATM switches) if there is some way to associate the input interface and VPI/VCI of ATM cells received with the output interface and VPI/VCI to be used on forwarding them. Typically this cannot be done in any interesting ATM switch router because VPI/VCI values on incoming and outgoing interfaces will correspond to the end stations or routers connected to these interfaces rather than to the source or destination of the IP packets being carried in the cells.

Folks at Toshiba recognized that if a signaling protocol were used to estab-lish new VPI/VCI values for specific flows of IP packets arriving at an input interface, then these special values could be bound to corresponding VPI/VCI values at an output interface. In this way a cell arriving with one VPI/VCI value could be switched at the ATM layer to the appropriate out-put interface and could be assigned the correct VPI/VCI for forwarding to the next hop router or end station. Yasuhiro Katsube, Ken-ichi Nagami, and Hiroshi Esaki submitted the Internet Draft "Router Architecture Extensions for ATM: Overview" to the IETF describing this idea in March 1995 ([CSR-E]).[8] In this draft, they proposed alternative signaling protocols and described how a cell switching router (CSR) could interwork with ATM switches, other types of ATM switch routers, and end stations.

The basic idea was that the majority of packet flows would still be processed using the routing function, but that specific flows would be for-warded at the ATM layer based on use of an additional signaling protocol. Flows involving special handling and flows consuming higher numbers of VCs would fall into two categories: default or dedicated VCs. Default VCs could be set up by using CLIP, for example. Dedicated VCs would be set up

---

8. References in square brackets are historical documents that have expired or been replaced by subsequent drafts. These references can be found in Table 2.4 at the end of this chapter.

using some other (in-band or out-of-band) signaling protocol. Protocols initially proposed for this purpose included Internet Stream Protocol version II (STII) and Reservation Protocol (RSVP). Subsequently, the same authors, along with four of their colleagues at Toshiba Research, proposed a specific protocol—Flow Attribute Notification Protocol (FANP)—in RFC 2129 (Nagami et al. 1996).

Kenji Fujikawa, of Kyoto University, published an Internet Draft ([IP-SVC]) in May 1996 that proposed a lightweight ATM signaling replacement for use within an ATM LIS. This was intended to replace CLIP as a complement to—and thus an extension of—the earlier CSR proposal. Although interest in this proposal continued for some time (it later became known as PLASMA), it has not become part of the mainstream effort in later MPLS standardization and signaling protocol development.

Ipsilon's IP Switching

Up to this point, existing proposals relied on use of native ATM signaling to establish at least default ATM virtual circuits. Ipsilon Networks suggested a new approach—abandon the currently defined signaling in ATM and introduce a new signaling protocol to be used to manage IP flows. Ipsilon proposed a flow management protocol (Ipsilon Flow Management Protocol, or IFMP) for use in establishing (for example) VPI/VCI values to be used by neighboring ATM switches for specific IP flows (Newman et al. 1996a). The assumption in this approach was that IP switches would forward IP packets between IP hosts and routers using default encapsulation[9] until a flow was detected and a redirection message sent. Once an IP switch sent a redirection message—including a new encapsulation value (VPI/VCI in ATM)—the neighboring host, router, or IP switch would forward packets belonging to the defined flow using the newly defined encapsulation. Use of the new data-link-layer encapsulation—which would be locally unique to a specific flow—would allow a neighboring router to forward IP packets associated with that flow at the data-link layer.

The Ipsilon approach had the advantage (relative to Toshiba's CSR proposal) of being potentially able to reduce the default-forwarding load by a

---

9. Using, for example, the well-known VPI/VCI 0/15 defined in RFC 1954 (Newman et al. 1996b) for encapsulating ATM AAL5 cells.

larger percentage of all IP packets being forwarded at any particular IP router. Unlike CSR, however, IFMP depended to a large degree on flow detection at each IP routing node in a network composed of IFMP-participating IP routers. This could result in significant overhead in IP packet processing in the default-forwarding mode and required implementations to pay attention to the activity of IP packets even in redirected flows.

In order to avoid the scale issues associated with both CLIP and NHRP, IFMP-participating implementations would need to use flow detection algorithms aimed at detecting a relatively small percentage of the total number of IP flows. In order to minimize the overall impact on IP forwarding, however, this small percentage of flows would need to carry a significant majority of the traffic. Based on data available from researchers at FIX-WEST,[10] folks at Ipsilon proposed several approaches for detecting flow that would result in low ratios of flow count to redirected packets.

The issues discussed relative to the Ipsilon approach were similar to those raised with CLIP and NHRP earlier, namely, the packet latency associated with protocol activity initiated by the prior existence of a flow of packets, and the scalability of the resulting virtual circuits in an ATM network of any appreciable size. As with NHRP, approaches that might reduce the latency would act to increase scaling issues, and vice versa.

In late March 1996, Greg Minshall of Ipsilon Networks observed that greater scalability was achievable through the use of ATM switches that could merge ATM cells at the frame level from multiple input VPI/VCIs onto a single output VPI/VCI.[11] This would have to be done without interleaving the cells associated with any particular frame with cells from other frames in the same output VPI/VCI. But it could be accomplished using a state variable—thus eliminating the need to actually assemble the frame at the IP layer. This simple observation may have led to the most significant contribution in many of the ensuing IP switching proposals. See Figure 2.1 for a time line of IP switching history.

---

10. The data referred to here was available from FIX-WEST. The analysis was presented publicly by Ipsilon and discussed extensively on the IP-ATM mailing list and at IETF meetings.

11. This observation was made on the IP-ATM mailing list in response to Juha Heinanen, specifically with respect to the inability of ATM switches to merge IP packet flows. Obviously, it is not possible to prove that this was the first public instance of this observation. However, it was at least an early instance.

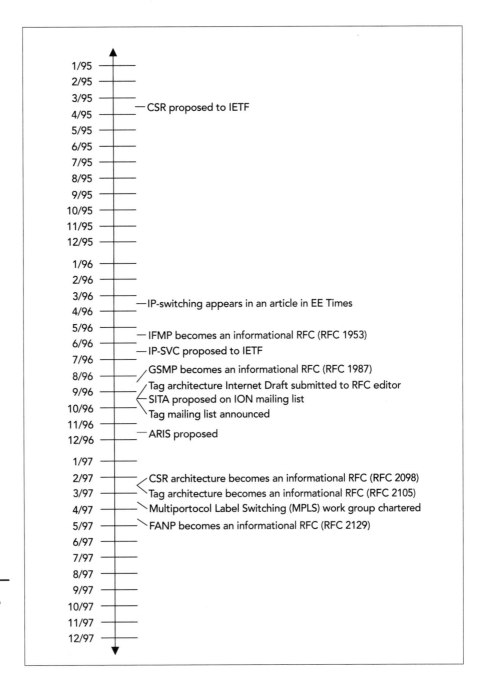

FIGURE 2.1

Time line for switching in IP up to the formation of the MPLS work group

2.2 Tag Switching, ARIS, and Other Proposals

In the last few months of 1996, several new proposals popped up either on the ROLC and ION mailing lists or on the mailing list set up by Cisco Systems to discuss their tag-switching proposal. Included among these were the following:

- Tag Switching, from Cisco Systems
- SITA (Switching IP through ATM), from Telecom Finland
- ARIS (Aggregate Route-based IP Switching), from IBM

Although it is clear that at least the initial tag-switching proposal was announced slightly earlier than the ARIS proposal, the ARIS proposal followed very shortly on the heels of the tag proposal. In addition, portions of the ARIS proposal covered material that was not found in the tag proposal until a couple of additional Internet Drafts were submitted.

Cisco Systems and IBM each publicly announced their own versions of IP switching late in 1996. Cisco announced the formation of a tag-switching discussion list and the availability of tag-switching architecture ([TAG-ARCH]) and Tag Distribution Protocol specification ([TDP]) documents in September. IBM posted an Internet Draft of their proposal ([ARIS]) in November. Cisco posted their first versions of tag switching over ATM and tag encapsulation in time for presentation at the December Birds of a Feather (BOF) meeting (IETF 1996).

The essential differences between the tag-switching and ARIS proposals were as follows.

- ARIS, although intended to apply to multiple media, focused on ATM and devoted an entire section to discussion of VC merging, whereas the tag architecture draft was written to apply generally.[12] (VC merging was implied by the assumption that the solution was scalable in the number of routes supported by the proposed architecture.
- ARIS introduced the concept of VP merging and the term *label*.
- The tag architecture and TDP drafts tied the assignment and advertisement of tags to local determination of a new route availability,

---

12. Tag switching and ARIS both eventually incorporated VC merging—certainly by the time that [TAG-ATM] version 1 came out.

whereas ARIS only allowed this to occur at an egress from a switching cloud.[13]

- The tag architecture document included alternative schemes for allocation of tags.

Both approaches included proposals for signaling the values to be used by peers in implementing the switching paradigm, and both relied on use of topology information from routing protocols to establish the paths to be used in packet switching. In addition, the tag-switching proposals added depth to the earlier CSR and IP switching proposals by providing alternatives for distribution of switching information. ARIS explicitly included proposals for dealing with scale concerns and looping paths.

Yet another proposal was discussed on the Internetworking over NBMA (ION) mailing list. This proposal—referred to at the time as Switching IP Through ATM [SITA]—suggested a simplistic configuration-based approach to supporting IP packet switching over ATM. It also suggested a variant of VP merging as later proposed in ARIS. In this proposal, ATM VCIs would be configured based on the egress for a specific class of packets, whereas VPIs would be configured based on the ATM ingress that first classified each packet. This proposal was updated in early November, but was subsequently dropped by its author.[14]

Although there had been an earlier attempt to establish a tag-switching forum, with the advent of tag switching, ARIS, and other proposals it was clear that the possibility of developing a standard packet-switching approach needed to be considered. Hence a BOF meeting was convened in December 1996. The result of this meeting was the decision to form an IETF working group, which would later come to be called the Multiprotocol Label Switching (MPLS) working group.

---

13. In ARIS, an egress point would assign and advertise VC labels on determination of a new route. The arrival of a new VC label advertisement, in association with an existing route advertisement, at a non-egress would trigger a like process until VC labels were advertised all the way to ingress points. This distinction grew into the choice of egress (ordered) control versus local (independent) control.

14. The author suggested fairly early on that SITA would be redundant if an explicit signaling protocol were to be defined. Since it subsequently became apparent that (at least one) such signaling protocol would be defined, perhaps this is the reason that the proposal was dropped.

2.3 An MPLS Working Group

Although the decision was made in December 1996 to form a working group to develop a standard approach for switching IP, the MPLS working group was not actually formed until March 3, 1997. Figure 2.2 shows both the projected and the actual schedule for delivery of MPLS specifications. It is apparent that the original projections were based on unbridled optimism in most cases. On average, the delay between hoped-for and actual delivery was more than one year.

To describe in detail how each of the various drafts developed by the MPLS working group evolved would take perhaps hundreds of pages and would therefore not be of use to most people. This chapter, however, attempts to capture pictorially how the numerous drafts were interrelated and to provide topical summaries of the evolution process. One general qualification must be made regarding this effort. I have tried to show reasonably strong links between drafts on related topics, based on specific acknowledgments,

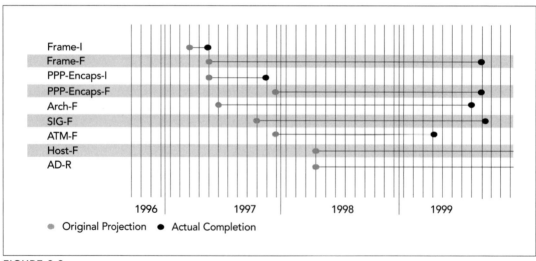

FIGURE 2.2

Scheduled versus actual MPLS working group goals. Frame-I, initial draft of MPLS framework; Frame-F, final draft of MPLS framework submitted to Internet Enginering Steering Group (IESG); PPP-Encaps-I, freeze additional input to PPP encapsulation; PPP-Encaps-F, final draft of PPP encapsulation submitted to IESG; Arch-F, final draft of MPLS architecture submitted to IESG; SIG-F, final draft(s) of label binding specifications to IESG; ATM-F, final draft(s) of ATM-specific MPLS to IESG; Host-F, final draft(s) of host behaviors to IESG; AD-R, review by AD (Area Director) and update schedule.

consensus of the working group (both on the mailing list and in working group meetings), and on participants in the process. It is necessary to acknowledge that other associations probably exist, and it is fair to admit that all drafts publicly issued at any given point may have had direct or indirect impact on the ideas and material that were included in subsequent drafts.

In addition, many of the drafts associated with development of MPLS signaling protocols were put forward either by individual contributors or by multiple contributors from individual organizations. Each section lists any design teams that are notable exceptions to this rule (for example, where members of more than one organization cooperated to develop one or more drafts). Note that the tables in this chapter list the affiliations of individuals contributing to each effort as they existed during the period of active work. For that reason, many of the individuals may be listed as having different affiliations in different efforts. Many have different affiliations now than during any part of the MPLS protocol development effort.[15]

Signaling Draft Development

Table 2.1 provides a list of design teams for various MPLS signaling specifications. Figure 2.3 depicts the interrelationships among the signaling documents discussed in this section.

LDP AND CR-LDP

Although several drafts contributed to development of the Label Distribution Protocol (LDP), the mainstream influence was from the combination of Cisco's initial Tag Distribution Protocol and IBM's ARIS proposals. At the end of 1997, [Exp-Rt] proposed specific information required to specify an explicit route in signaling. This proposal led to inclusion of significant new text in the LDP specification in the early part of 1998 for support of explicit routes. Because of other efforts that were in progress at the time, the consensus of the working group was that LDP would go forward more quickly if explicit route setup of label-switched paths was specified in a separate draft. This was done in middle to late 1998 by creating a new draft, [CR-LDP-0], and removing explicit route support from the LDP specification.

---

15. This has been humorously referred to as the "engineer shift-left" phenomenon.

TABLE 2.1. Signaling Design Teams

Team	Member(s)	Affiliation(s)
LDP Design	Loa Andersson	Ericsson Telecom, Bay Networks, Nortel Networks
	Paul Doolan	Ennovate Networks
	Nancy Feldman	IBM
	Andre Fredette	Bay Networks, Nortel Networks
	Bob Thomas	Cisco Systems
CR-LDP Design	Osama Aboul-Magd, Loa Andersson, Peter Ashwood-Smith, Andre Fredette, Bilel Jamoussi	Nortel Networks
	Ross Callon	Ironbridge Networks
	Ram Dantu, Liwen Wu	Alcatel
	Paul Doolan	Ennovate Networks
	Nancy Feldman	IBM
	Joel Halpern	Newbridge Networks
	Juha Heinanen	Telia Finland
	Fiffi Hellstrand, Kenneth Sundell	Ericsson Telecom
	Timothy Kilty	Northchurch Communications
	Andrew Malis	Ascend Communications
	Muckai Girish	SBC Technology Resources
	Pasi Vaananen	Nokia Telecommunications
	Tom Worster	General DataComm
MPLS-RSVP Design	Bruce Davie, Yakov Rekhter, Eric Rosen	Cisco Systems
	Arun Viswanathan	Lucent Technologies
	Vijay Srinivasan, Steven Blake	IBM
RSVP-TE Design	Daniel Awduche	UUNET Worldcom
	Lou Berger	Fore Systems
	Der-Hwa Gan, Tony Li	Juniper Networks
	George Swallow	Cisco Systems
	Vijay Srinivasan	Torrent Networks
Loop Prevention Design	Yoshihiro Ohba, Yasuhiro Katsube	Toshiba
	Eric Rosen	Cisco Systems
	Paul Doolan	Ennovate Networks

LDP, Label Distribution Protocol; CR-LDP, Constraint-based Routing LDP; MPLS-RSVP, MPLS with Reservation Protocol; RSVP-TE, extensions to RSVP for traffic engineering.

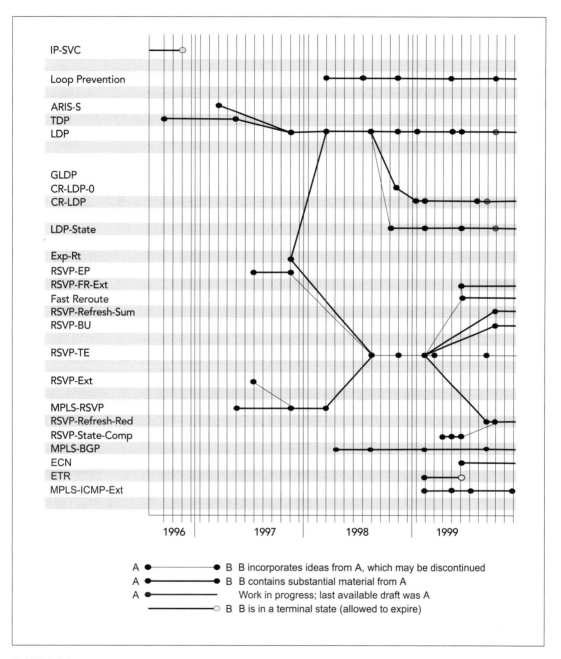

IP-SVC
Loop Prevention
ARIS-S
TDP
LDP

GLDP
CR-LDP-0
CR-LDP

LDP-State

Exp-Rt
RSVP-EP
RSVP-FR-Ext
Fast Reroute
RSVP-Refresh-Sum
RSVP-BU

RSVP-TE

RSVP-Ext

MPLS-RSVP
RSVP-Refresh-Red
RSVP-State-Comp
MPLS-BGP
ECN
ETR
MPLS-ICMP-Ext

1996   1997   1998   1999

A ●————————● B   B incorporates ideas from A, which may be discontinued
A ●————————● B   B contains substantial material from A
A ●————————   Work in progress; last available draft was A
————————○ B   B is in a terminal state (allowed to expire)

FIGURE 2.3

Signaling document road map (see Table 2.4 for key to abbreviations)

At this same time, a concern was raised about potential confusion of state machine interactions between LDP implementations using different control and label allocation modes in setting up LSPs. This was of particular concern because of the separation of signaling of explicit routes from the base Label Distribution Protocol specification. The working group established a draft ([LDP-State]) on LDP state machines for LSP setup to provide information on these interactions.

Both the LDP and CR-LDP drafts reached a state of relative completion in late 1999, and [LDP-State] entered working group last call toward the end of 1999. With the exception of modifying the procedures in appendices (to support nonmerging LSPs) in the LDP specification, all LDP-related drafts received only minor editing changes throughout the year 2000.

RSVP AND RSVP-TE

Multiple proposals for piggybacking MPLS labels in the Integrated Services Reservation Protocol (RSVP) messages emerged in mid to late 1997. These were merged into a single working group draft ([MPLS-RSVP]) that then became the basis for development of [RSVP-TE] in the second half of 1998. [RSVP-TE] incorporated ideas from [Exp-Rt] and [MPLS-RSVP] in a series of drafts describing how the RSVP signaling protocol could be used to establish LSPs for traffic engineering tunnels. Throughout the later part of 1998, several concerns were raised regarding well-known scaling limitations with the RSVP signaling protocol; many of these concerns were addressed in [RSVP-TE] in early 1999. At that time, several issues were raised regarding the proposed modifications for improved scalability and reliability, and these features—along with a proposal for fast LSP rerouting—were moved into separate drafts. The drafts on improved RSVP scalability and reliability were then moved to the RSVP working group for consideration as generalized improvements in RSVP. [RSVP-TE] reached a state of relative completion in late 1999, receiving only minor editing changes throughout the year 2000.

OTHER SIGNALING PROPOSALS

Proposals for Explicit Congestion Notification ([ECN]) and extensions to Internet Control Message Protocol (ICMP) ([MPLS-ICMP-Ext]) were determined by the Area directors to be of more general applicability than specifically to MPLS and are now being worked on orthogonally to the MPLS specification effort. As of mid-2000, Explicit Tree Route ([ETR]) is no longer active, and both [MPLS-BGP] and [Loop Prevention] await publication as RFCs (the former as a proposed standard RFC and the latter as an experimental RFC).

Encapsulation and Related Draft Development

Table 2.2 lists the design teams for MPLS encapsulation efforts. Figure 2.4 illustrates the interrelationships among the various encapsulation drafts.

For the most part, the evolution of encapsulation was fairly simple. There were a few proposals that, although potentially influential in other ways, never directly became a part of the mainstream effort—for example, SITA and IPSOFACTO. Other efforts that were specifically asked for in framework and architecture specification documents apparently lost energy (for example, ships in the night operation [MPLS-SIN] and VP switching).

TABLE 2.2. Encapsulation Design Teams

Team	Member(s)	Affiliation(s)
PPP/Ethernet Encapsulation	Eric Rosen, Yakov Rekhter, Daniel Tappan, Dino Farinacci	Cisco Systems
	Tony Li	Juniper Networks
	Alex Conta	Lucent Technologies, 3Com
MPLS-ATM Design	Bruce Davie, Jeremy Lawrence, Keith McCloghrie, Yakov Rekhter, Eric Rosen, George Swallow	Cisco Systems
	Paul Doolan	Ennovate Networks
MPLS-FR Design	Alex Conta	Lucent Technologies
	Paul Doolan	Cisco Systems, Ennovate Networks
	Andrew Malis	Ascend Communications, Lucent Technologies

PPP, Point-to-Point Protocol; MPLS-ATM, MPLS over ATM; MPLS-FR, MPLS over Frame Relay.

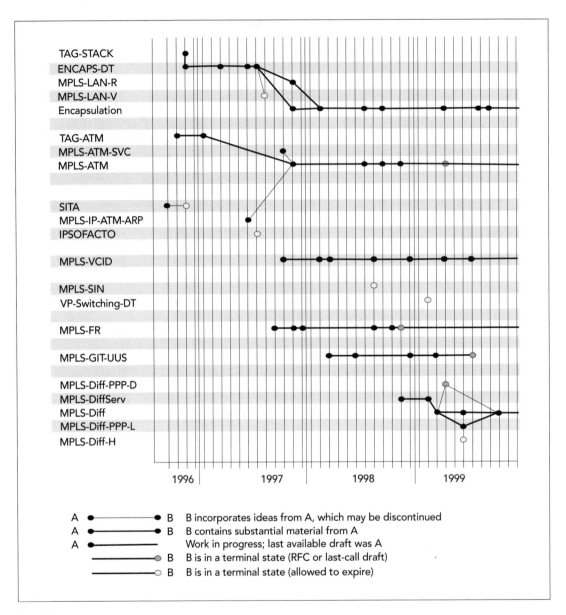

FIGURE 2.4

Encapsulation document road map (see Table 2.4 for key to abbreviations)

Two exceptions to this orderly progression, shown in Figure 2.4, were the following issues:

- Separation of LAN encapsulation from the generic and PPP encapsulation draft ([Encapsulation]), and the subsequent merging of the two separate resulting drafts ([MPLS-LAN-R] and [Encapsulation]).[16]

- Separation of the specification of ATM and Frame Relay Differentiated Services from PPP Differentiated Services. Two PPP Differentiated Service drafts were proposed separately ([MPLS-Diff-PPP-L] and [MPLS-Diff-PPP-D]), and both were recombined in the mainstream differentiated service draft, [MPLS-Diff]. The major influence came from [MPLS-Diff-PPP-L] rather than [MPLS-Diff-PPP-D].

Frame Relay specification reached a state of relative completion toward the end of 1998, as did ATM specification in mid-1999. Generic LAN and PPP encapsulation and Differentiated Services were essentially complete toward the end of 1999.

Framework, Architecture, and Other General Draft Development

Table 2.3 lists the design teams for MPLS framework and architecture. Figure 2.5 provides a visual map of the development and relationships among the various drafts.

MPLS architecture evolved from the combination of [ARIS] and [TAG-ARCH]. Cisco's tag-switching architecture and Toshiba's cell-switching architecture both became informational RFCs in early 1997, and related architectural proposals to the MPLS working group were discontinued.

MPLS architecture, framework, and three applicability statements ([CR-LDP-App], [LDP-App], and [RSVP-TE-App]) reached effective completion in the second half of 1999.

---

16. The draft [MPLS-LAN-V] was dropped after a comparison was presented in December 1997. One major concern raised was the need to assign values for use in LAN encapsulation that would preserve proper functioning of existing learning bridge implementations.

TABLE 2.3. Framework and Architecture Design Teams

Team	Member(s)	Affiliation(s)
Framework	Ross Callon	Cascade Communications, Ascend Communications, Ironbridge Networks
	Paul Doolan	Cisco Systems, Ennovate Networks
	Nancy Feldman	IBM
	Andre Fredette	Bay Networks, Nortel Networks
	George Swallow	Cisco Systems
	Arun Viswanathan	IBM, Lucent Technologies
Architecture	Eric Rosen	Cisco Systems
	Arun Viswanathan	IBM, Lucent Technologies
	Ross Callon	Cascade Communications, Ascend Communications, Ironbridge Networks

Virtual Private Networks, Traffic Engineering, and Optimized Multipathing Draft Development

A number of attempts to kick-start an effort to include standardization of an approach for virtual private network (VPN) support were made in the MPLS working group as well as in the IETF in general. The main reason the majority of the VPN proposals were tabled is that the requirements for VPN functionality were felt to be a subset of the requirements for traffic engineering (TE). Exceptions were a proposal to support VPNs over MPLS using BGP ([BGP-MPLS-VPN]) and a proposal for a standard VPN identifier format ([VPN-ID]). Both of these proposals are now RFCs.

The draft that energized much of the work in the MPLS working group from mid-1998 through late 1999 was the traffic engineering requirements document ([TER]). This draft—endorsed as it was by a major user of networking equipment—very quickly became the centerpiece for virtually all efforts in signaling and other areas of MPLS development. It became an RFC in the second half of 1999.

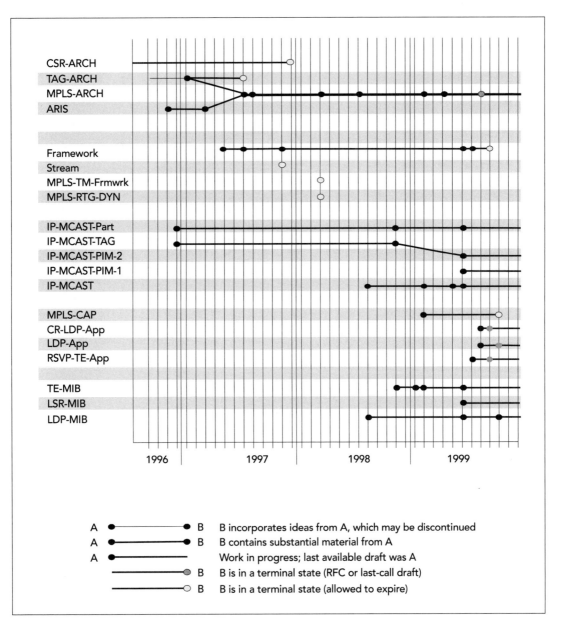

FIGURE 2.5

Architecture, framework, and issues document road map (see Table 2.4 for key to abbreviations)

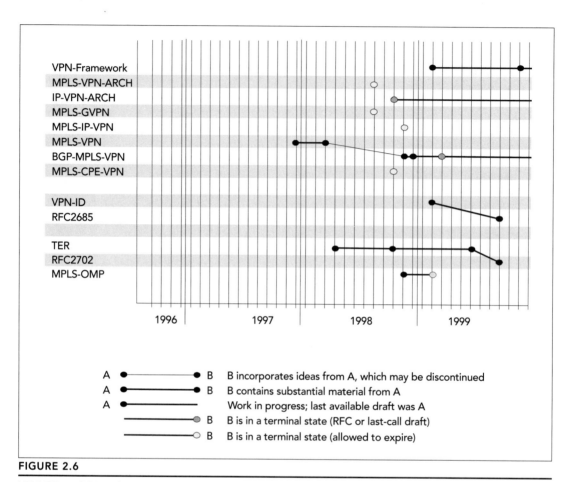

FIGURE 2.6

VPN, TE, and OMP document road map (see Table 2.4 for key to abbreviations)

Although there was genuine interest in optimized multipathing (OMP) from several IETF working groups,[17] the author of the draft on this topic was its primary driver in the MPLS working group. However, there was no consensus that there was a need to define anything in an MPLS context, and this draft was allowed to expire.

Figure 2.6 summarizes the development and relationships of the drafts on VPN, TE, and OMP.

---

17. Optimized multipathing proposals similar to the one brought to the MPLS working group were also brought to the ISIS and OSPF working groups (which are also in the Routing Area) and were accepted as working group drafts.

The references listed in this chapter are divided into two categories: (1) Internet Drafts that have expired or been replaced by subsequent drafts or RFCs, as well as other historical documents as referred to by figures in this chapter, and (2) the usual references to current and available publications. Table 2.4 lists the references in the first category. Note that Internet Drafts are by their nature "works in progress." This table of Internet Drafts is for historical purposes and is not intended to indicate that the listed documents are useful as reference material for determining how these ideas are actually implemented or should be implemented.

Because of the IETF's policy of archiving expired or superseded drafts, many of these drafts are not available at IETF ftp sites. However, Internet Drafts are frequently archived by individuals who want to be able to trace the evolution of the ideas in a series of Internet Drafts. Most may be obtainable from one or more of the original authors as well. I would like to extend a special thanks to Noritoshi Demizu of Sony Computer Science Laboratory for having archived a few of the drafts that I was missing at his Multi-Layer Routing site, http://infonet.aist-nara.ac.jp/member/nori-d/mlr/id. Having these drafts at my disposal allowed me to verify dates and other information required to complete this chapter.

References

ATM Forum. 1997a (July). LAN emulation over ATM, version 2—LUNI specification. AF-LANE-0084.000. Available at ftp://ftp.atmforum.com/pub/approved-specs/af-lane-0084.000.

ATM Forum. 1997b (July). Multi-protocol over ATM, version 1.0. AF-MPOA-0087.000. Available at ftp://ftp.atmforum.com/pub/approved-specs/af-mpoa-0087-000.

Awduche, Daniel O., Joe Malcolm, Johnson Agogbua, Mike O'Dell, and Jim McManus. 1999 (September). Requirements for traffic engineering over MPLS. RFC 2702. Available at http://www.isi.edu/in-notes/rfc2702.txt.

Fox, Barbara A., and Bryan Gleeson. 1999 (September). Virtual private networks identifier. RFC 2685. Available at http://www.isi.edu/in-notes/rfc2685.txt.

Gleeson, Bryan, Arthur Lin, Juha Heinanen, Grenville Armitage, and Andrew G. Malis. 2000 (February). A framework for IP based virtual private networks. RFC 2764. Available at http://www.isi.edu/in-notes/rfc2764.txt.

Heinanen, Juha. 1999 (September). Multiprotocol encapsulation over ATM Adaptation Layer 5. RFC 2684. Available at http://www.isi.edu/in-notes/rfc2684.txt.

Internet Engineering Task Force (IETF). 1996. Proceedings of the thirty-seventh Internet Engineering Task Force, San Jose, California, December 9–13. Available at http://www.ietf.org/proceedings/96dec/toc-96dec.html.

Internet Engineering Task Force (IETF). 1997a. Proceedings of the thirty-eighth Internet Engineering Task Force, Memphis, Tennessee, April 7–11. Available at http://www.ietf.org/proceedings/97apr/97apr-final/httoc.htm.

Internet Engineering Task Force (IETF). 1997b. Proceedings of the thirty-ninth Internet Engineering Task Force, Munich, Germany, August 11–15. Available at http://www.ietf.org/proceedings/97aug/toc-97aug.html.

Internet Engineering Task Force (IETF). 1997c. Proceedings of the fortieth Internet Engineering Task Force, Washington, DC, December 8–12. Available at http://www.ietf.org/proceedings/97dec/index.html.

Internet Engineering Task Force (IETF). 1998a. Proceedings of the forty-first Internet Engineering Task Force, Los Angeles, California, March 30–April 3. Available at http://www.ietf.org/proceedings/98mar/index.html.

Internet Engineering Task Force (IETF). 1998b. Proceedings of the forty-second Internet Engineering Task Force, Chicago, Illinois, August 23–28. Available at http://www.ietf.org/proceedings/98aug/index.html.

Internet Engineering Task Force (IETF). 1998c. Proceedings of the forty-third Internet Engineering Task Force, Orlando, Florida, December 7–11. Available at http://www.ietf.org/proceedings/98dec/index.html.

Internet Engineering Task Force (IETF). 1999a. Proceedings of the forty-fourth Internet Engineering Task Force, Minneapolis, Minnesota, March 15–19. Available at http://www.ietf.org/proceedings/99mar/index.html.

Internet Engineering Task Force (IETF). 1999b. Proceedings of the forty-fifth Internet Engineering Task Force, Oslo, Norway, July 11–16. Available at http://www.ietf.org/proceedings/99jul/index.html.

Internet Engineering Task Force (IETF). 1999c. Proceedings of the forty-sixth Internet Engineering Task Force, Washington, DC, November 7–12. Available at http://www.ietf.org/proceedings/99nov/index.html.

Internet Engineering Task Force (IETF). 2000. Proceedings of the forty-seventh Internet Engineering Task Force, Adelaide, Australia, March 26–31. Available at http://www.ietf.org/proceedings/00mar/index.html.

Katsube, Yasuhiro, Ken-ichi Nagami, and Hiroshi Esaki. 1997 (February). Toshiba's router architecture extensions for ATM: overview. RFC 2098. Available at http://www.isi.edu/in-notes/rfc2098.txt.

Laubach, Mark. 1998 (April). Classical IP and ARP over ATM. RFC 2225. Available at http://www.isi.edu/in-notes/rfc2225.txt.

Luciani, James, Dave Katz, David Piscitello, Bruce Cole, and Naganand Doraswamy. 1998 (April). NBMA Next Hop Resolution Protocol (NHRP). RFC 2332. Available at http://www.isi.edu/in-notes/rfc2332.txt.

Maher, Maryann. 1998 (April). ATM signaling support for IP over ATM—UNI signalling 4.0 update. RFC 2331. Available at http://www.isi.edu/in-notes/rfc2331.txt.

Nagami, Ken-ichi, Yasuhiro Katsube, Yasuro Shobatake, Akiyoshi Mogi, Shigeo Matsuzawa, Tatsuya Jinmei, and Hiroshi Esaki. 1996 (November). Toshiba's Flow Attribute Notification Protocol (FANP) specification. RFC 2129. Available at http://www.isi.edu/in-notes/rfc2129.txt.

Newman, Peter, W. L. Edwards, Robert Hinden, Eric Hoffman, Fong Ching Liaw, Tom Lyon, and Greg Minshall. 1996a (May). Ipsilon Flow Management Protocol specification for IPv4 version 1.0. RFC 1953. Available at http://www.isi.edu/in-notes/rfc1953.txt.

Newman, Peter, W. L. Edwards, Robert Hinden, Eric Hoffman, Fong Ching Liaw, Tom Lyon, and Greg Minshall. 1996b (May). Transmission of flow labelled IPv4 on ATM data links Ipsilon version 1.0. RFC 1954. Available at http://www.isi.edu/in-notes/rfc1954.txt.

Perez, Maryann, Fong Ching Liaw, Allison Mankin, Eric Hoffman, Dan Grossman, and Andrew Malis. 1995 (February). ATM signaling support for IP over ATM. RFC 1755. Further augmented by RFC 2331. Available at http://www.isi.edu/in-notes/rfc1755.txt and http://www.isi.edu/in-notes/rfc2331.txt.

Rekhter, Yakov, Bruce Davie, Dave Katz, Eric Rosen, and George Swallow. 1997 (February). Cisco Systems' tag switching architecture overview. RFC 2105. Available at http://www.isi.edu/in-notes/rfc2105.txt.

Rosen, Eric, and Yakov Rekhter. 1999 (March). BGP/MPLS VPNs. RFC 2547. Available at http://www.isi.edu/in-notes/rfc2547.txt.

Waldrop, M. Mitchell. 1992. *Complexity: The Emerging Science at the Edge of Order and Chaos*. New York: Simon and Schuster.

TABLE 2.4 Historical Internet Drafts and RFCs

Key	Version	Date	Authors*	Title
[ARIS]	0 basic 0 overview	11/1996 3/1997	R. Boivie, N. Feldman, A. Viswanathan, R. Woundy	*ARIS: Aggregate Route-Based IP Switching* draft-woundy-aris-ipswitching-00 and draft-viswanathan-aris-overview-00
[ARIS-S]	0	3/1997	N. Feldman, A. Viswanathan	*ARIS Specification* draft-feldman-aris-spec-00
[BGP-MPLS-VPN]	0 1 2547 0 1 2	11/1998 12/1998 3/1999 3/2000 5/2000 7/2000	E. Rosen, Y. Rekhter, T. Bogovic, R. Vaidyanathan, S. Brannon, M. Morrow, M. Carugi, C. Chase, T. Wo Chung, J. De Clercq, E. Dean, P. Hitchin, M. Leelanivas, D. Marshall, L. Martini, V. Srinivasan	*BGP/MPLS VPNs* draft-rosen-vpn-mpls-00 and 01, RFC2547 and draft-rosen-rfc2547bis-00 through 02
[CLIP]	1577 2225	1/1994 4/1998	M. Laubach	*Classical IP and ARP over ATM* RFC1577 and RFC2225
[COCIFO-ATM]	0	10/1994	H. Esaki, K. Nagami, M. Ohta	*Connection Oriented and Connectionless* *IP Forwarding over ATM Networks* draft-esaki-co-cl-ip-forw-atm-00
[CR-LDP]	0 1 2 3 4	1/1999 2/1999 8/1999 9/1999 7/2000	B. Jamoussi (Ed.)	*Constraint-Based LSP Setup Using LDP* draft-ietf-mpls-cr-ldp-00 through 04
[CR-LDP-0]	0	10/1998	L. Andersson, A. Fredette, B. Jamoussi, R. Callon, R. Dantu, P. Doolan, N. Feldman, M. Girish, E. Gray, J. Halpern, J. Heinanen, T. Kilty, A. Malis, K. Sundell, P. Vaananen, T. Worster, L. Wu	*Constraint-Based LSP Setup Using LDP* draft-jamoussi-mpls-cr-ldp-00
[CR-LDP-APP]	0 0 1	8/1999 9/1999 7/2000	G. Ash, M. Girish, E. Gray, B. Jamoussi, G. Wright	*Applicability Statement for CR-LDP* draft-jamoussi-mpls-crldp-applic-00 draft-ietf-mpls-crldp-applic-00 and 01

Key	Number	Date	Authors	Title
[CSR]	2098	2/1997	Y. Katsube, K. Nagami, H. Esaki	*Toshiba's Router Architecture Extensions for ATM: Overview* RFC2098
[CSR-ARCH]	0	12/1997	Y. Katsube, K. Nagami, Y. Ohba, S. Matsuzawa, H. Esaki	*Cell Switch Router—Architecture and Protocol Overview* draft-katsube-csr-arch-00
[CSR-E]	0	3/1995	Y. Katsube, K. Nagami, H. Esaki	*Router Architecture Extensions for ATM: Overview* draft-katsube-router-atm-overview-00
[ECN]	0	6/1999	K. Ramakrishnan, S. Floyd, B. Davie	*A Proposal to Incorporate ECN in MPLS* draft-ietf-mpls-ecn-00
[ENCAPS-DT]	0 1 2 3	11/1996 3/1997 6/1997 7/1997	E. Rosen, Y. Rekhter, D. Tappan, D. Farinacci, G. Fedorkow, T. Li, A. Conta	*Label Switching: Label Stack Encodings* draft-rosen-tag-stack-00 through 03
[Encapsulation]	0 1 2 3 4 5 6 7 8	11/1997 2/1998 7/1998 9/1998 4/1999 8/1999 9/1999 9/1999 7/2000	E. Rosen, Y. Rekhter, D. Tappan, D. Farinacci, G. Fedorkow, T. Li, A. Conta	*MPLS Label Stack Encoding* draft-ietf-MPLS-label-encaps-00 through 08
[ETR]	0 1	2/1999 6/1999	H. Hummel, S. Loke	*Explicit Tree Routing* draft-hummel-mpls-explicit-tree-00 and 01
[Exp-Rt]	0	11/1997	B. Davie, T. Li, E. Rosen, Y. Rekhter	*Explicit Route Support in MPLS* draft-davie-mpls-explicit-routes-00
[FANP]	2129	11/1996	K. Nagami, Y. Katsube, Y. Shobatake, A. Mogi, S. Matsuzawa, T. Jinmei, H. Esaki	*Toshiba's Flow Attribute Notification Protocol (FANP) Specification* RFC2129

continued

TABLE 2.4 *Continued*

Key	Version	Dates	Authors*	Title
[Fast-Reroute]	0 1 2 3 4	6/1999 6/1999 12/1999 3/2000 5/2000	D. Haskin, R. Krishnan	*A Method for Setting an Alternative Label Switched Path to Handle Fast Reroute* draft-haskin-mpls-fast-reroute-00 through 04
[FLIP]	1954	5/1996	P. Newman, W. Edwards, R. Hinden, E. Hoffman, F. Liaw, T. Lyon, G. Minshall	*Transmission of Flow Labelled IPv4 on ATM Data Links Ipsilon Version 1.0* RFC1954
[Framework]	0 1 2 3 4 5	5/1997 7/1997 11/1997 6/1999 7/1999 9/1999	R. Callon, N. Feldman, A. Fredette, G. Swallow, P. Doolan, A. Viswanathan	*A Framework for Multiprotocol Label Switching* draft-ietf-mpls-framework-00 through 05
[GLDP]	0	11/1997	E. Gray, G. Armitage, Z. Wang	*Generic Label Distribution Protocol Specification* draft-gray-mpls-generic-ldp-spec-00
[IFMP]	1953	5/1996	P. Newman, W. Edwards, R. Hinden, E. Hoffman, F. Liaw, T. Lyon, G. Minshall	*Ipsilon Flow Management Protocol Specification for IPv4 Version 1.0* RFC1953
[IP-MCAST]	0 1 2 0 1	8/1998 2/1999 5/1999 6/1999 5/2000	D. Ooms, W. Livens, B. Sales, M. Ramalho, A. Acharya, F. Griffoul, F. Ansari	*Framework for IP Multicast in MPLS* draft-ooms-mpls-multicast-00 through 02 draft-ietf-mpls-multicast-00 and 01
[IP-MCAST-Part]	0 0 1	12/1996 11/1998 9/1999	D. Farinacci, Y. Rekhter	*Partitioning Tag Space among Multicast Routers on a Common Subnet* draft-farinacci-multicast-tag-part-00 and *Partitioning Label Space among Multicast Routers on a Common Subnet* draft-multicast-label-part-00 and 01

Key	Version	Date	Authors	Title
[IP-MCAST-PIM-1]	0	11/1998	W. Livens, D. Ooms, B. Sales	*MPLS for PIM-SM* draft-ooms-mpls-pimsm-00
[IP-MCAST-PIM-2]	0	6/1999	D. Farinacci, Y. Rekhter, E. Rosen	*Using PIM to Distribute MPLS Labels for Multicast Routes* draft-farinacci-mpls-multicast-00
[IP-MCAST-TAG]	0 1	12/1996 11/1998	D. Farinacci, Y. Rekhter	*Multicast Tag Binding and Distribution Using PIM and Multicast Label Binding and Distribution Using PIM* draft-farinacci-multicast-tagsw-00 and 01
[IPSOFACTO]	0	7/1997	A. Acharya, R. Dighe, F. Ansari	*IPSOFACTO: IP Switching over Fast ATM Cell Transport* draft-acharya-ipsw-fast-cell-00
[IP-SVC]	0 1	5/1996 11/1996	K. Fujikawa	*Another ATM Signaling Protocol for IP* (see also [PLASMA]) draft-fujikawa-ipsvc-00 and 01
[IP-VPN-ARCH]	0 0 1 2 3	10/1998 1/2000 5/2000 5/2000 6/2000	K. Muthukrishnan, A. Malis	*Core IP VPN Architecture* draft-muthukrishnan-corevpn-arch-00 and *Core MPLS IP VPN Architecture* draft-muthukrishnan-mpls-corevpn-arch-00 through 03
[LANE]	2	1997	J. Keene (Ed.)	*LAN Emulation Over ATM, Version 2—LUNI Specification* ATM Forum Technical Committee
[LDP]	0 0 1 2 3 4 5 6 7	11/1997 3/1998 8/1998 11/1998 1/1999 5/1999 6/1999 10/1999 6/2000	L. Andersson, P. Doolan, N. Feldman, A. Fredette, R. Thomas	*LDP Specification* draft-feldman-ldp-spec-00 and draft-ietf-mpls-ldp-00 through 10

continued

TABLE 2.4 *Continued*

Key	Version	Date	Authors*	Title
[LDP], *continued*	8	6/2000		
	9	8/2000		
	10	8/2000		
[LDP-APP]	0	8/1999	R. Thomas, E. Gray	*LDP Applicability*
	0	10/1999		draft-thomas-mpls-ldp-applic-00 and
	1	6/2000		draft-ietf-mpls-ldp-applic-00 through 02
	2	8/2000		
[LDP-MIB]	0	8/1998	J. Cucchiara, H. Sjostrand, J. Luciani	*Definitions of Managed Objects for the*
	1	6/1999		*Multiprotocol Label Switching, Label*
	2	10/1999		*Distribution Protocol (LDP)*
	3	10/1999		draft-ietf-mpls-ldp-mib-00 through 06
	4	1/2000		
	5	3/2000		
	6	7/2000		
[LDP-State]	0	10/1998	L. Wu, P. Cheval, C. Boscher,	*LDP State Machine*
	0	2/1999	E. Gray	draft-wu-mpls-ldp-state-00 and
	1	6/1999		draft-ietf-mpls-ldp-state-00 through 03
	2	10/1999		
	3	1/2000		
[Loop-Prevention]	0	3/1998	Y. Ohba, Y. Katsube, E. Rosen,	*MPLS Loop Prevention Mechanism Using*
	1	7/1998	P. Doolan	*LSP-id and Hop Count*
	2	11/1998		draft-ohba-mpls-loop-prevention-00 and
	0	5/1999		*MPLS Loop Prevention Mechanism*
	1	5/1999		draft-ohba-mpls-loop-prevention-01, 02
	2	10/1999		and draft-ietf-mpls-loop-prevention-00
	3	4/2000		through 03

Tag	No.	Date	Authors	Title / Draft
[LSR-MIB]	0	6/1999	C. Srinivasan, T. Nadeau, A. Viswanathan	*MPLS Label Switch Router Management Information Base Using SMIv2* draft-ietf-mpls-lsr-mib-00 through 06
	1	2/2000		
	2	3/2000		
	3	4/2000		
	4	5/2000		
	5	7/2000		
	6	7/2000		
[MPLS-ARCH]	0	7/1997	E. Rosen, A. Viswanathan, R. Callon	*A Proposed Architecture for MPLS* draft-rosen-mpls-arch-00 and *Multiprotocol Label Switching Architecture* draft-ietf-mpls-arch-01 through 07
	1	3/1998		
	2	7/1998		
	3	2/1999		
	4	2/1999		
	5	4/1999		
	6	8/1999		
	7	7/2000		
[MPLS-ATM]	0	11/1997		*Use of Label Switching with ATM* draft-davie-mpls-atm-00 and 01 and draft-ietf-mpls-atm-00, and *MPLS Using LDP and ATM VC Switching* draft-ietf-mpls-atm-01 through 04
	1	7/1998		
	0	9/1998		
	1	11/1998		
	2	4/1999		
	3	5/2000		
	4	6/2000		
[MPLS-ATM-SVC]	0	10/1997	N. Demizu, K. Nagami, P. Doolan, H. Esaki	*ATM SVC Support for ATM-LSRs* draft-demizu-mpls-atm-svc-00
[MPLS-BGP]	0	4/1998	Y. Rekhter, E. Rosen	*Carrying Label Information in BGP-4* draft-ietf-mpls-bgp4-mpls-00 through 04
	1	8/1998		
	2	2/1999		
	3	9/1999		
	4	1/2000		
[MPLS-CAP]	0	2/1999	L. Andersson, B. Jamoussi, M. Girish, T. Worster	*MPLS Capability Set* draft-loa-mpls-cap-set-00 and 01

continued

TABLE 2.4 *Continued*

Key	Version	Date	Authors*	Title
[MPLS-CPE-VPN]	0	10/1998	T. Li	*CPE Based VPNs Using MPLS* draft-li-mpls-vpn-00
[MPLS-Diff]	0	3/1999	F. le Faucheur, L. Wu, B. Davie,	*MPLS Support of Differentiated Services by ATM LSRs and Frame Relay LSRs*
	1	6/1999	S. Davari, P. Vaananen,	draft-ietf-mpls-diff-ext-00 and 01
	2	10/1999	R. Krishnan, P. Cheval, J. Heinanen	*MPLS Support of Differentiated Services*
	3	2/2000		draft-ietf-mpls-diff-ext-02 through 07
	4	3/2000		
	5	6/2000		
	6	7/2000		
	7	8/2000		
[MPLS-Diff-H]	0	6/1999	J. Heinanen	*Differentiated Services in MPLS Networks* draft-heinanen-diffserv-mpls-00
[MPLS-Diff-PPP-D]	0	4/1999	S. Davari, R. Krishnan, P. Vaananen	*MPLS Support of Differentiated Services over PPP Links* draft-davari-mpls-diff-ppp-00
[MPLS-Diff-PPP-L]	0	6/1999	F. le Faucheur, S. Davari, R. Krishnan, P. Vaananen, B. Davie	*MPLS Support of Differentiated Services over PPP Links* draft-lefaucheur-mpls-diff-ppp-00
[MPLS-DiffServ]	0	11/1998	L. Wu, P. Cheval, P. Vaananen,	*MPLS Extensions for Differential Services* draft-wu-mpls-diff-ext-00 and 01
	1	2/1999	F. le Faucheur, B. Davie	
[MPLS-FR]	0	9/1997	A. Conta, P. Doolan, A. Malis	*Use of Label Switching with Frame Relay Specification*
	1	11/1997		draft-conta-mpls-fr-00 and
	0	12/1997		*Use of Label Switching on Frame Relay Networks Specification*
	1	8/1998		draft-conta-mpls-fr-01 and
	2	10/1998		draft-ietf-mpls-fr-00 through 06
	3	11/1998		
	4	5/2000		
	5	6/2000		
	6	6/2000		

Reference	Date	#	Authors	Title
[MPLS-GIT-UUS]	6/1998 12/1998 3/1999 7/1999 1/2000	0 1 2 3 4	M. Suzuki	*The Assignment of the Information Field and Protocol Identifier in the Q.2941 Generic Identifier and Q.2957 User-to-User Signaling for the Internet Protocol* draft-ietf-mpls-git-uus-00 through 04
[MPLS-GVPN]	8/1998	0	J. Heinanen, B. Gleeson	*MPLS Mappings of Generic VPN Mechanisms* draft-heinanen-generic-vpn-mpls-00
[MPLS-ICMP-Ext]	2/1999 5/1999 7/1999 12/1999 8/2000	0 1 0 1 2	R. Bonica, D. Tappan, D. Gan	*ICMP Extensions for MultiProtocol Label Switching* draft-bonica-icmp-mpls-00, 01 and draft-ietf-mpls-icmp-00 through 02
[MPLS-IP-ATM-ARP]	7/1997	0	H. Esaki, Y. Katsube, K. Nagami, P. Doolan, Y. Rekhter	*IP Address Resolution and ATM Signaling for MPLS over ATM SVC Services* draft-katsube-mpls-over-svc-00
[MPLS-IP-VPN]	11/1998	0	L. Casey, I. Cunningham, R. Eros	*IP VPN Realization Using MPLS Tunnels* draft-casey-vpn-mpls-00
[MPLS-LAN-R]	11/1997	0	E. Rosen, Y. Rekhter, D. Tappan, D. Farinacci, G. Fedorkow, T. Li, A. Conta	*MPLS Label Stack Encoding on LAN Media* draft-rosen-mpls-lan-encaps-00
[MPLS-LAN-V]	8/1997	0	D. Bussiere, H. Esaki, A. Ghanwani, S. Matsuzawa, J. Pace, V. Srinivasan	*Labels for MPLS over LAN Media* draft-srinivasan-mpls-lans-label-00
[MPLS-OMP]	11/1998 2/1999	0 1	C. Villamizar	*MPLS Optimized Multipath (MPLS-OMP)* draft-villamizar-mpls-omp-00 and 01
[MPLS-RSVP]	5/1997 11/1997 3/1998	0 1 0	B. Davie, Y. Rekhter, E. Rosen, A. Viswanathan, V. Srinivasan, S. Blake	*Use of Label Switching with RSVP* draft-davie-mpls-rsvp-00 and 01, and draft-ietf-mpls-rsvp-00
[MPLS-RTG-DYN]	3/1998	0	S. Ayandeh, Y. Fan	*MPLS Routing Dynamics* draft-ayandeh-mpls-dynamics-00

continued

TABLE 2.4 *Continued*

Key	Version	Date	Authors*	Title
[MPLS-SIN]	0	8/1998	B. Jamoussi, N. Feldman, L. Andersson	*MPLS Ships in the Night Operation with ATM* draft-jamoussi-mpls-sin-00
[MPLS-TM-Frmwrk]	0	3/1998	P. Vaananen, R. Ravikanth	*Framework for Traffic Management in MPLS Networks* draft-vaananen-mpls-framework-00
[MPLS-VCID]	1 0 0 1 2 3 4 5	10/1997 2/1998 3/1998 8/1998 12/1998 4/1999 7/1999 8/2000	K. Nagami, N. Demizu, H. Esaki, Y. Katsube, P. Doolan	*VCID Notification over ATM Link* draft-demizu-mpls-vcid-atm-01, draft-nagami-mpls-vcid-atm-00, and draft-ietf-mpls-vcid-atm-00 through 03 *VCID Notification over ATM Link for LDP* draft-ietf-mpls-vcid-atm-04 and 05
[MPLS-VPN]	0 1	12/1997 3/1998	J. Heinanen, E. Rosen	*VPN Support with MPLS* draft-heinanen-mpls-vpn-00 and 01
[MPLS-VPN-ARCH]	0	8/1998	D. Jamieson, B. Jamoussi, G. Wright, P. Beaubien	*MPLS VPN Architecture* draft-jamieson-mpls-vpn-00
[MPOA]	1	1997	A. Fredette (Ed.)	*Multi-Protocol over ATM, Version 1.0* ATM Forum Technical Committee
[NHRP]	2332	4/1998	J. Luciani, D. Katz, D. Piscitello, B. Cole, N. Doraswamy	*NBMA Next Hop Resolution Protocol (NHRP)* RFC2332
[PLASMA]	0	3/1997	K. Fujikawa	*Point-to-point Link Assembly for Simple Multiple Access (PLASMA)* draft-fujikawa-plasma-00
[RFC1483]	1483 2684	7/1993 9/1999	J. Heinanen, D. Grossman	*Multiprotocol Encapsulation over ATM Adaptation Layer 5* RFC1483 and RFC2684

Key	Number	Date	Authors	Title
[RFC1755]	1755	2/1995	M. Perez, F. Liaw, A. Mankin, E. Hoffman, D. Grossman, A. Malis	*ATM Signaling Support for IP over ATM* RFC1755, augmented by RFC2331
[RFC2105]	2105	9/1996	Y. Rekhter, B. Davie, D. Katz, E. Rosen, G. Swallow	*Cisco Systems' Tag Switching Architecture Overview* RFC2105
[RFC2331]	2331	4/1998	M. Maher	*ATM Signaling Support for IP over ATM—UNI Signalling 4.0 Update* RFC2331
[RFC2547]	2547	3/1999	E. Rosen, Y. Rekhter	*BGP/MPLS VPNs* RFC2547
[RFC2684]	2684	9/1999	J. Heinanen, D. Grossman	*Multiprotocol Encapsulation over ATM Adaptation Layer 5* RFC2684
[RFC2685]	2685	9/1999	B. Fox, B. Gleeson	*Virtual Private Networks Identifier* RFC2685
[RFC2702]	2702	7/1999	D. Awduche, J. Malcolm, J. Agogbua, M. O'Dell, J. McManus	*Requirements for Traffic Engineering over MPLS*
[RFC2764]	2764	2/2000	B. Gleeson, A. Lin, J. Heinanen, G. Armitage, A. Malis	*A Framework for IP Based Virtual Private Networks* RFC2764
[RSVP Aggregation]	0	11/1997	R. Guerin, S. Blake, S. Herzog	*Aggregating RSVP-based QoS Requests* draft-guerin-aggreg-rsvp-00
[RSVP-ATM]	0	6/1999	W. Wimer	*MPLS Using RSVP and ATM Switching* draft-wimer-mpls-atm-rsvp-00
[RSVP-BU]	0	10/1999	R. Goguen, G. Swallow	*RSVP Label Allocation for Backup Tunnels* draft-swallow-rsvp-bypass-label-00
[RSVP-CIDR Aggregation]	1	6/1997	J. Boyle	*RSVP Extensions for CIDR Aggregated Data Flows* draft-ietf-rsvp-cidr-ext-01

continued

TABLE 2.4 *Continued*

Key	Version	Date	Authors*	Title
[RSVP-EP]	0	7/1997	D. Gan, R. Guerin, S. Kamat, T. Li, E. Rosen	*Setting Up Reservations on Explicit Paths Using RSVP* draft-guerin-expl-path-rsvp-00 and 01
	1	11/1997		
[RSVP-Ext]	0	7/1997	A. Viswanathan, V. Srinivasan, S. Blake	*Soft State Switching: A Proposal to Extend RSVP for Switching RSVP Flows* draft-viswanathan-mpls-rsvp-00
[RSVP-FR-Ext]	0	6/1999	R. Krishnan, D. Haskin	*Extensions to RSVP to Handle Establishment of Alternative Label-Switched Paths for Fast Re-route* draft-ietf-rsvp-refresh-reduct-00 and 01
	1	6/1999		
[RSVP-Refresh-Red]	0	9/1999	L. Berger, D. Gan, G. Swallow, P. Pan, F. Tommasi, S. Molendini	*RSVP Refresh Reduction Extensions* draft-ietf-rsvp-refresh-reduct-00 through 05
	1	10/1999		
	2	1/2000		
	3	3/2000		
	4	4/2000		
	5	6/2000		
[RSVP-Refresh-Sum]	0	10/1999	G. Swallow	*RSVP Hierarchical Summary Refresh* draft-swallow-rsvp-hierarchical-refresh-00
[RSVP-State-Comp]	0	4/1999	L. Wang, A. Terzis, L. Zhang	*A Proposal for Reducing RSVP Refresh Overhead Using State Compression* draft-wang-rsvp-state-compression-00 *RSVP Refresh Overhead Reduction by State Compression* draft-wang-rsvp-state-compression-01 and 02
	1	5/1999		
	2	6/1999		
[RSVP-TE]	0	8/1998	D. Awduche, L. Berger, D. Gan, T. Li, G. Swallow, V. Srinivasan	*Extensions to RSVP for Traffic Engineering* draft-swallow-mpls-rsvp-trafeng-00 *Extensions to RSVP for LSP Tunnels* draft-ietf-mpls-rsvp-lsp-tunnel-00 through 04 *RSVP-TE: Extensions to RSVP for LSP Tunnels*
	0	11/1998		
	1	2/1999		
	2	3/1999		
	3	9/1999		
	4	9/1999		
	5	2/2000		

Tag	#	Date	Authors	Reference
	6	7/2000		draft-ietf-mpls-rsvp-lsp-tunnel-05 through 07
	7	8/2000		
[RSVP-TE-APP]	0	7/1999	D. Awduche, A. Hannan, X. Xiao	*Applicability Statement for Extensions to RSVP for LSP-Tunnels*
	1	9/1999		draft-awduche-mpls-rsvp-tunnel-applicability-00 and 01 and draft-ietf-mpls-rsvp-tunnel-applicability-00 and 01
	0	9/1999		
	1	4/2000		
[RSVP-TE-DT]	0	8/1998	D. Awduche, D. Gan, T. Li, G. Swallow, V. Srinivasan	*Extensions to RSVP for Traffic Engineering* draft-swallow-mpls-rsvp-trafeng-00
[SITA]	0	9/1998	J. Heinanen	*Switching IP through ATM*
	1	11/1998		ION e-mail discussion
[Stream]	0	11/1997	A. Fredette, C. White, L. Andersson, P. Doolan	*Stream Aggregation* draft-fredette-mpls-aggregation-00
[TAG-ARCH]	0	1/1997	Y. Rekhter, B. Davie, D. Katz, E. Rosen, G. Swallow, D. Farinacci	Tag Switching Architecture—Overview draft-davie-tag-switching-atm-00 and 01
	1	7/1997		
[TAG-ATM]	0	10/1996	B. Davie, P. Doolan, J. Lawrence, K. McCloghrie, Y. Rekhter, E. Rosen, G. Swallow	*Use of Tag Switching with ATM* draft-davie-tag-switching-atm-00 and 01
	1	1/1997		
[TAG-CSR]	0	4/1997	Y. Ohba, H. Esaki, Y. Katsube	*Comparison of Tag Switching and Cell Switch Router* draft-ohba-tagsw-vs-csr-00
[TAG-STACK]	0	11/1996	E. Rosen, D. Tappan, D. Farinacci, Y. Rekhter, G. Fedorkow	*Tag Switching: Tag Stack Encodings* draft-rosen-tag-stack-00
[TDP]	0	9/1996	P. Doolan, B. Davie, D. Katz, Y. Rekhter, E. Rosen	*Tag Distribution Protocol* draft-doolan-tdp-spec-00 and 01
	1	5/1997		
[TE-MIB]	0	11/1998	C. Srinivasan, A. Viswanathan, T. Nadeau	*MPLS Traffic Engineering Management Information Base* draft-srinivasan-mpls-te-mib-00 and 01 *MPLS Traffic Engineering Management*
	1	1/1999		
	0	2/1999		
	1	6/1999		

continued

TABLE 2.4 *Continued*

Key	Version	Date	Authors*	Title
[TE-MIB], *continued*	3	3/2000		*Information Base Using SMIv2*
	4	7/2000		draft-ietf-mpls-te-mib-00, 01, 03, and 04
[TER]	0	4/1998	D. Awduche, J. Malcolm,	*Requirements for Traffic Engineering over*
	0	10/1998	J. Agogbua, M. O'Dell, J. McManus	*MPLS*
	1	6/1999		draft-awduche-mpls-traffic-eng-00
				draft-ietf-mpls-traffic-eng-00 and 01
[VPN-Framework]	1	2/1999	B. Gleeson, A. Lin, J. Heinanen,	*A Framework for IP Based Virtual Private*
	3	11/1999	G. Armitage, A. Malis	*Networks*
				draft-gleeson-vpn-framework-01 and 03
[VPN-ID]	0	2/1999	B. Fox, B. Gleeson	*Virtual Private Networks Identifier*
[VP-Switching-DT]	0	2/1999	N. Feldman, B. Jamoussi,	*MPLS Using ATM VP Switching*
			S. Komandur, A. Viswanathan,	draft-feldman-mpls-atmvp-00
			T. Worster	

For entries with multiple versions listed, the Authors column lists all authors for all versions, beginning with the lead author of the first draft listed.

3

FRAMEWORK

3.1 Requirements

MPLS has three broad requirements, which are discussed in this chapter:

- Relationship to routing
- Relationship to network-layer protocols
- Relationship to link-layer protocols

Relationship to Routing

MPLS forwarding mechanisms operate independently of routing. To maximize the compatibility of the MPLS packet-forwarding technology with route determination mechanisms (including existing routing protocols, routing extensions, future routing protocols, and other means of determining the route that an identified set of packets will follow), it is highly desirable that the basic forwarding technology is defined in such a way as to be as decoupled from the route determination process as possible. Figure 3.1 shows a typical interface arrangement between route determination functions (routing protocol engine, policy management, filtering, etc.) and packet-forwarding mechanisms. MPLS should minimize the complexity of the required interface in terms of the quantity of information exchange required to set up and forward packets.

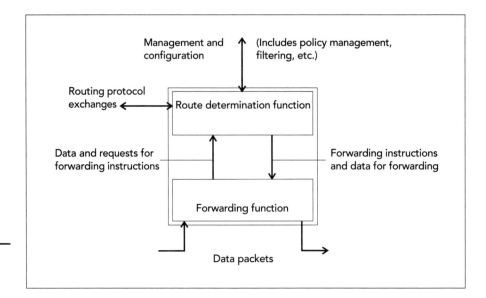

FIGURE 3.1

Separation of
routing and
forwarding

In general, a route determination function can offload a subset of its tasks,
allowing a corresponding subset of packets to be forwarded without query-
ing the route determination function for each packet processed.[1] Alternatively, the information provided to the forwarding function can allow this
function to perform some portion of the routing decision, reducing the
burden on the route determination function and possibly allowing for
pipelining or parallel processing of the remaining routing decision process.
Offloading the entire route determination process to the forwarding function may not be practical when the forwarding decision is based on arbitrary bit locations in the data packets being forwarded. When this is the
case, some subset of the decision-making process would still need to be
done directly by the route determination function.

This process involves an engineering trade-off between the amount of
packet forwarding that can be done by the forwarding function without
direct involvement of the route determination function and the complexity
of the forwarding function itself. One measure of the complexity of the
forwarding function is how likely it is that the forwarding function imple-

---

1. The subset of route determination tasks can be either in a form that can be directly used
by the forwarding function or in a form that can be translated to such a form.

mentation is affected by new requirements in route determination (such as new requirements for packet filtering, a change in the way packets are processed, and so on). New requirements of this type occur quite often and may be driven by such uncontrollable influences as discovery of some additional security measures required to avoid a new form of attack.[2]

By defining mechanisms by which the data that is significant to the route determination process can be abbreviated using a fixed-length label, MPLS makes it possible for any individual implementation to realize an optimal trade-off, with considerably more of the forwarding decisions being made in a relatively uncomplicated forwarding function—often with minimal change in the implementation's architecture.

Note that MPLS does not excuse the entire networking system from ever having to make a route determination based on the potentially complex route determination function (using arbitrary bit positions in received data). The process of negotiating (or distributing) labels pushes this task to the MPLS implementation(s) that will serve as ingress for a particular stream of data packets (matching the criteria that would have been used to make the route determination at each router in the absence of MPLS). However, only the ingress will typically need to make this determination once a label-switched path (LSP) has been established.

The normal mode for MPLS is to forward packets following the path determined by routing. The wording settled on by the members of the MPLS working group responsible for defining an MPLS framework was to the effect that MPLS integrates label switching and routing at the network layer. In an interesting twist of meaning, this equates to decoupling (dis-integration) of the binding between route determination and forwarding, since MPLS—and the label-switching paradigm in particular—is expected to make it easier to extend the route determination process by providing this decoupling effect.

As shown in Figure 3.1, routing protocols (and other routing functions, such as static routes, policies, and filtering) drive the route determination process. Although some internetworking features (notably, use of explicit routes) may be a great deal more practical when using MPLS, the essential

---

2. Security is not covered in this book. In general, attacks can take several forms, and new attacks are discovered about as often as new defenses are designed for existing attacks.

orientation of the route determination process remains the same when using MPLS as it is when using routers without MPLS—that is to say, routing still drives the route determination process.

Where route determination might be performed on a per-packet basis for a significant subset of all packets forwarded in a non-MPLS router, MPLS allows the determination to be made at the time labels are being negotiated between MPLS implementations. The route determination function drives both the process of associating labels with a forwarding equivalence class (FEC) and of injecting label associations[3] into the forwarding information base (FIB). The route determination function also drives the process of removing label associations.

MPLS should perform better and in a larger network environment than an equivalent routing solution. This is expected to come about as an evolutionary process. The degree to which this actually occurs depends on a number of factors, including the following:

- The extent to which the ability of routing devices to make routing decisions gains on dominant wire speeds in the Internet in overall deployment, without MPLS

- The extent to which MPLS capabilities become ubiquitous in routing or administrative domains, or both

- The extent to which MPLS supports, and is used for, tunneling applications

The first of these factors tends to reduce the degree to which MPLS offers an improvement in the performance of individual network devices with increasing availability of wire-speed routers. The second factor tends to increase the overall network performance to the extent that the capability is available on individual network devices. The second and third factors

---

3. A label association, in this context, may be an FEC and an output label (or label stack if multiple labels are added) and interface at the ingress; an input interface and label (or label stack if one or more pop operations take place) and an output label (or label stack if one or more push operations take place) and interface at an intermediate LSR; or an input interface and label (or label stack if more than one pop operations occur) and an output interface at the egress.

together tend to increase the ability of the network to scale to larger sizes to the extent that MPLS is available and supports tunneling.

WIRE-SPEED ROUTING

As MPLS has been evolving, several companies have announced products that offer wire-speed routing at gigabit and even terabit wire speeds. Improvements in the process of making routing decisions make it possible to obtain the performance MPLS promises without the need to develop a new standard technology. In fact, the existence of routers demonstrating these levels of packet-processing ability may lead to the perception that MPLS is an unnecessary complication since it introduces a new type of packet to process in such devices.[4]

The extent to which MPLS is not needed or may add costs and delays (as a result of additional complexity in the product) in providing packet processing at wire speeds also affects the degree to which MPLS might become ubiquitous in a network routing or administrative domain.

UBIQUITY

Figure 3.2 shows a partial MPLS deployment in a relatively simplistic network. In this network, isolated MPLS devices are unable to realize any advantage over standard routing because they are effectively the ingress and egress for every LSP that might be established through them. With small clusters of MPLS devices—consisting of two or three LSRs—the benefit obtained from using MPLS over the relatively small number of links and the relatively small percentage of total recognizable FECs that can be assigned to an LSP may not outweigh the costs associated with signaling and processing labels. It is not until relatively large (section diameter greater than or equal to 3) cut-sections of a network are entirely populated with LSRs that you're likely to see a reduction in the average amount of

---

4. This thinking could be used to demonstrate another advantage of decoupling the route determination and forwarding functions: Implementing the forwarding function for this new packet type will be simpler because the interface to the forwarding function is made simpler by using labels. However, this argument is circular.

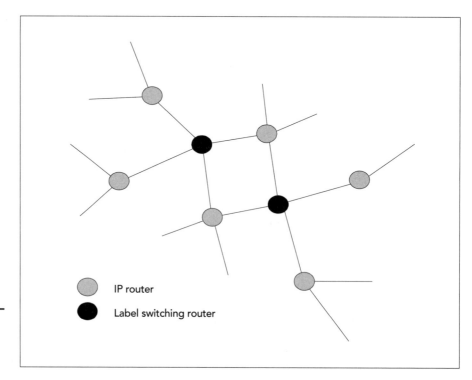

FIGURE 3.2

Partial deployment of label switching routers

work done at each LSR. Note that even under these circumstances there may be no actual gain in performance in the network.

TUNNELING

MPLS forwarding is controlled by the route determination function at LSP setup time. This route determination function itself participates in routing protocols. A routing entity that is part of an LSR is not (by virtue of this fact alone) intrinsically capable of successfully maintaining peer relationships with a larger number of other routing entities than a routing entity that is not part of an LSR. Consequently, there is nothing terribly obvious about MPLS that makes it possible for LSRs to perform in a larger network environment than other routers.

What does make this possible is that labels can be used—possibly in a hierarchical fashion via label stacking—to establish tunnels (peer-to-peer, explicitly routed, etc.). Tunnels are already used as an approach to overcome addressing and scaling problems in the Internet today (see Chapter 6). MPLS labels consume less space in packet headers than many other tunneling approaches and can be established more easily (possibly using relatively complex instructions that would be prohibitively difficult to implement in standard routing but that are feasible in MPLS because of the separation of route determination and forwarding).

MPLS tunnels can be used to improve the utilization of the network through traffic engineering (see Traffic Engineering in Chapter 7), making it possible to build larger networks with fewer problems such as network hot spots and underutilization. MPLS tunnels can also be used to virtualize networks (see Virtual Private Networks in Chapter 7) such that the route determination function is not required to maintain peer relationships with as many routers.

Relationship to Network-Layer Protocols

MPLS will initially support Internet Protocol version 4 (IPv4) (Postel 1981) but be extensible for support of IPv6 and possibly other network-layer protocols and addressing schemes. MPLS is intended to be able to support multiple layer 3 (L3 or network-layer) protocols (hence the name Multiprotocol Label Switching). Initially, however, the focus of the effort is on defining system components and functions required to support IPv4.

Support for additional network-layer protocols requires specification of protocol-specific FECs and required extensions to MPLS protocols for associating labels with these new FECs. The specification would need to include additional messages, message contents, and processing behaviors and would need to account for behaviors relating to looping data, control messages, and interactions with routing, among other things. The existing specifications already define FECs for IPv6 network-layer addressing, for example, but do not address interactions between MPLS and IPv6 routing (for good reasons—these interactions are not yet fully defined).

Note that—again, because of the separation of route determination and forwarding—these additional specification requirements do not affect implementations of the MPLS forwarding function. This is a highly significant factor in potential MPLS support of additional network-layer protocols because reducing the impact on highly optimized forwarding functions increases the ease with which additional support can be provided.

Relationship to Link-Layer Protocols

MPLS should not be restricted to any particular link layer. Specification of MPLS operation over various media is required in order to realize many of the intended benefits of MPLS. Currently, the specified media support includes ATM, Frame Relay, and generic MPLS shim (for PPP and Ethernet). See Encapsulation in Chapter 6 for media-specific details.

3.2 Benefits

Simple Forwarding Paradigm

Forwarding is based on an exact match of a relatively small, fixed-length field (a label) as opposed to (for example) a longest match on a similar-length field, or a complicated evaluation of arbitrary bit positions in an arbitrary-length portion of data packets being forwarded. This section discusses the benefits of using MPLS as a forwarding paradigm. Not all of the benefits apply in every case. It has even been argued that several of these benefits have been overcome by technological developments. The actual length of the label is media and session specific. See Encapsulation in Chapter 6 for media-specific details.

Explicitly Routed LSPs

Explicit routes are established as LSPs. It is not necessary to include and evaluate an explicit route with each packet forwarded. See Explicit-Route Tunnels in Chapter 6 for more information on this topic.

Traffic Engineering

The ability to explicitly route a portion of the data traffic along paths not normally used by standard routing (for example, not the optimal path chosen by an interior gateway protocol) makes it possible to realize greater control in engineering traffic flow across a network. Mechanisms for accomplishing this function in the absence of MPLS involve configuration of routing metric values, static routes, and (using, for example, ATM or Frame Relay) permanent virtual circuits. This configuration is typically done either manually or under the control of a management system. Determination of the traffic that will be rerouted is typically done using an offline path and resource computation on a weekly or possibly daily basis. This is frequently referred to as offline traffic engineering. Traffic engineering based on explicit routes allows the network administrator to use arbitrary flow granularity and potentially a much smaller time scale to obtain more efficient utilization and minimize congestion in the network. See Traffic Engineering in Chapter 7 for a more detailed discussion.

Quality of Service

Allocation of special treatment facilities for packets associated with an FEC that is to receive some form of preferential treatment is done at LSP setup. In addition, it is possible to perform policing and traffic shaping at ingress to an LSP (as opposed to at each hop). Quality of Service: Premium Services in Chapter 7 addresses this topic in greater detail.

Even if it is desirable to support a less state-full quality-of-service (QoS) model—such as that defined for Differentiated Services—use of an essentially connection-oriented signaling model allows the network to perform sanity checks to determine if the capacity to provide a service exists prior to committing to provision of that service.

Work Partitioning

The process of assigning packets of a particular FEC to an LSP is done once at the ingress of the LSP, rather than at each hop. The process of signaling, or negotiating, label and FEC associations allows core network devices to push the task of packet classification toward the edge of the network.

In cases where edgeward devices have substantial packet-forwarding capability using L3 as well as MPLS, it is even possible to share the packet classification task among edgeward LSRs by forwarding a portion of the traffic at L3 to be classified by LSRs further downstream.

The packet classification process is easily partitioned using hierarchical LSPs as well. An example of where this is useful is when an edge-to-edge service requires LSPs to classify and process packets as individual streams. By aggregating tributary streams as they progress toward the core of the network, and deaggregating them as they progress away from the core, it is possible to classify and treat individual packet streams on the basis of an extremely fine granularity. Higher-level LSPs may be treated as fixed-capacity pipes, allowing fine-grained treatment of individual packet streams in lower-level LSPs.

Routing Protocol Scalability

MPLS offers increased scalability of routing protocols by reducing the number of peer relationships that a routing entity is required to maintain. MPLS provides mechanisms for virtualizing network topology, thus allowing routers in virtual networks to maintain a peer relationship only with routers in that same virtual network. In addition, MPLS defines system behavior in such a way that it is not necessary to have full-mesh peer relationships in a hybrid switching and routing network environment.

This concept requires some more explanation. Intuitively, it would seem that tunneling between routing peers results in more peer relationships. This is a commonly recurring theme in discussion of overlay and peer routing models. However, it is possible to partition an implementation into separate routing instances such that one routing instance deals with local peers in order to route tunnels to remote peers while another routing instance deals with a set of remote peers. Partitioning the overall routing problem in this manner is a good way to reduce the complexity associated with dealing with local and remote peers. This partitioning is very similar to that used in gateway routers that need to deal with remote exterior gateway protocol (EGP) and local interior gateway protocol (IGP) peers.

Common Signaling

The same label distribution techniques are usable over ATM, Frame Relay, Ethernet, PPP, and other media. Thus deployment of MPLS applications (such as traffic engineering or VPNs) is possible across multiple media types, using common signaling.

Simplified Management

Because MPLS allows applications to be deployed over multiple media using common signaling and forwarding mechanisms, management of the network in support of these applications is greatly simplified.

Reduced Latency

Using a topology-driven approach to establish LSPs for normal, best-effort forwarding of data packets virtually eliminates latency in packet transport. Setup of LSPs driven directly by routing transactions should result in availability of an LSP nearly as quickly as a route is available.[5] Because packets would not be deliverable in the absence of an available route, the additional latency is very small generally or—in the case where a piggyback label distribution mechanism is used—nonexistent.

References

Callon, Ross, Nancy Feldman, Paul Doolan, Andre Fredette, George Swallow, and Arun Viswanathan. A framework for Multiprotocol Label Switching; a work in progress.

Postel, Jon, ed. 1981 (September). Internet Protocol. RFC 791. Available at http://www.ietf.org/rfc/rfc0791.txt.

---

5. The ability to successfully establish topology-driven LSPs for all known routes depends to a very large degree on the presence of merge-capable LSRs in the MPLS network.

4

ARCHITECTURE

A doctor can bury his mistakes, but an architect can only advise his client to plant vines.
•*Frank Lloyd Wright*

4.1 MPLS System Components

 MPLS as a system relies on the concepts of Label Switching Router (LSR), Label-Switched Path (LSP), and labeled packets. In its simplest form, MPLS is the concept of LSRs forwarding labled packets on LSPs. This section describes these components in more detail.

Label Switching Router

This section describes the components that make up a label switching router.

FORWARDING INFORMATION BASE

The MPLS architecture document (Rosen, Viswanathan, and Callon 2001) defines the components of the forwarding information base (FIB)[1] as follows:

- Next Hop Label Forwarding Entry (NHLFE): An entry containing next-hop information (interface and next-hop address) and label

---

1. A forwarding information base is an analogue for a router's routing information base. It contains information necessary to forward a labeled packet.

manipulation[2] instructions; it may also include label encoding, L2 encapsulation information, and other information required for processing packets in the associated stream.

- Incoming Label Map (ILM): A mapping from incoming labels to corresponding NHLFEs.
- FEC-to-NHLFE map (FTN): A mapping from the FEC of any incoming packets to corresponding NHLFEs.

It is important to note that this is a reasonable, but arbitrary, division of the tasks that are performed in a FIB lookup, based on the local LSR's role in any LSP. An actual implementation may, for example, internally classify unlabeled packets and assign an internal label. This would permit the implementation to include a label as part of each NHLFE to be used as a key in accessing successive matching NHLFEs. Note also that the existence of more than one matching NHLFE may be a function of the label retention mode (discussed later in this chapter) and whether or not the local LSR is supporting multipathing[3] or multicast LSPs.

How the required NHLFE is accessed depends on the role the LSR plays in the specific LSP: If the LSR is the ingress, it uses an FTN; otherwise, it uses an ILM.

ROUTE DETERMINATION MODULE

The route determination function is used to construct FIB entries in the normal mode of MPLS operation. Information from routing protocol interactions determines FECs for which it is desirable to create an NHLFE, as well as the next-hop information needed to construct the NHLFE. Because MPLS currently only defines downstream allocation[4] of labels, an NHLFE will not contain an output (downstream) label until a label has been allocated by the downstream peer LSR.

---

2. See the section Label Stack Manipulation later in this chapter.

3. Multipathing is the process of distributing packets destined for the same network egress across multiple paths. The general topic of how this would be done is not discussed in this book.

4. Labels are allocated for upstream interfaces and distributed to upstream peers from downstream LSRs. See Label Allocation Modes later in this chapter for a more complete explanation.

The LSR constructs NHLFEs by one of the following methods:

- Allocating one or more labels to be used as the incoming label, creating ILMs for each, binding each ILM to the set of NHLFEs, and distributing the labels allocated to upstream LSRs

- Creating FTNs for FECs associated with specific routing entries and binding each to a set of NHLFEs with corresponding next-hop information

Note that an NHLFE that does not contain a downstream label will either have a pop label manipulation instruction or a drop forwarding instruction.[5] For this reason, it does not make sense to create an NHLFE associated with an FTN and without a downstream label.

The route determination function is also used to remove (or update) FIB entries when, for instance, routes associated with a given FEC are removed or next-hop information is changed.

FORWARDING MODULE

The forwarding function in MPLS is based on a simple exact match of a label to an ILM, which in turn maps to an NHLFE. The LSR follows the label manipulation instructions of the NHLFE and delivers the packet to the interface specified in the next-hop information. The LSR may also need to use L2 encapsulation information provided in the NHLFE to properly encapsulate the packet for delivery to the correct next hop.[6]

In the event that the matched ILM maps to more than one NHLFE, the specific behavior is determined based on the context within which multiple NHLFEs were created. One NHLFE may be selected based on associated

---

5. As defined in the MPLS architecture Internet Draft (Rosen, Viswanathan, and Callon 2001), labels are contained in an NHLFE in the form of a label manipulation instruction. This is yet another way in which implementations may elect not to follow the architectural model exactly. For instance, an implementation may use one set of labels (in the form of a label stack) to match an NHLFE/FIB entry that itself contains zero or more labels (again, in stack form), which would be used to replace the labels used to locate the NHLFE/FIB entry.

6. This would likely be the case with an Ethernet link, where the MAC (media access control) address of the output interface and the next-hop router must be included in the Ethernet encapsulation in order to deliver the packet to the next hop. Some implementations may also choose to include the protocol number so that the output interface hardware does not have to determine on its own whether the packet is labeled.

preference values among multiple NHLFEs (if, for example, each additional NHLFE is used to provide a redundant LSP or to support load sharing). Multiple NHLFEs may be used (if multicasting data, for instance). Hence, the behavior in the event that a single ILM maps to multiple NHLFEs depends on why the LSR allowed a second, and each subsequent, NHLFE to be created.

Figure 4.1 shows the decision tree for the forwarding function using PPP links as an example. The PPP Protocol field is used to determine whether the LSR is looking for an ILM (protocol number 0x0281 or 0x0283)[7] or an FTN (various other protocol numbers).[8] The ILM or FTN is then used to find at least one NHLFE, which is then used to determine the output interface, label manipulation instructions, and related forwarding information. A very similar decision tree would apply to Ethernet links (using Ether type values 0x8847 or 0x8848).[9] The decision tree for ATM or Frame Relay is simpler because the label is incorporated in the L2 header itself, eliminating the need to evaluate a higher-level protocol identifier at L2.

Label-Switched Path

This section describes the components that make up a label-switched path.

INGRESS, EGRESS, INTERMEDIATE, AND TRANSPARENT

At ingress to an LSP, an LSR pushes at least one label onto the label stack. Label(s) pushed onto the label stack may be the first label(s) in the stack.

In this case, we know that the NHLFE that contained the label manipulation instructions used to push the label(s) onto the stack was located using an FTN and that the local LSR may be an ingress to MPLS generally.[10]

---

7. 0x0281 and 0x0283 are protocol numbers defined for MPLS (unicast and multicast, respectively) in PPP (Rosen et al. 2000).

8. See IANA (Undated b) for applicable Protocol field numbers. Several of these numbers are applicable to PPP Link Control, Quality Monitoring, MPLS Control, and various other PPP control protocols and would thus be exempt from forwarding. In implementations, however, none of these protocol types would make it to this point in a forwarding decision tree.

9. Values for Ether type may be obtained from IANA (Undated a).

10. There is at least one (mildly strange) case in which a packet arrives at an LSR's input interface from another LSR, unlabeled and not as a direct result of L3 standard routing. This occurs when the upstream LSR has popped the last label on the label stack as a penultimate hop pop, only to have the local LSR push a new label onto the label stack. In this case,

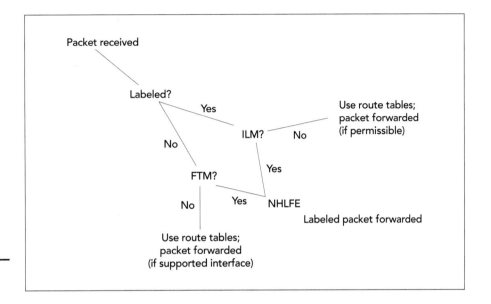

FIGURE 4.1

Forwarding
decision tree

An LSR that pops at least one label off the label stack is either the egress or
the penultimate hop for the LSP. The distinction between penultimate hop
and egress is a small one when both pop a label. In fact, for LSRs that can
terminate an LSP at an output interface, the distinction is essentially nonexistent. An LSR that performs a simple label swap is an intermediate LSR.

Labels in the label stack below[11] those changed by label manipulation
instructions correspond to LSPs for which the local LSR is transparent.

In the independent control mode,[12] an LSP for which the local LSR is an
egress may be spliced together with another LSP for which it is the
ingress.[13] Where it would have popped one label and pushed another, it
now swaps one label for the other. In this case, the LSR has become an
intermediate LSR with respect to the concatenated LSP.

An implementation may allow for fairly complex label manipulation
instructions in an NHLFE (for example, pop one or more labels and then

---

the packet did not arrive as a direct result of L3 routing because it was forwarded from a
particular interface based on an NHFLE in the upstream LSR.

11. Labels that occur after other labels in the encapsulation are said to be *below* them in the
label stack.

12. See Control Modes, later in this chapter.

13. *Splicing* is the process of binding an ILM to an NHLFE.

push one or more labels). This LSR may splice LSPs for which it is the egress at multiple levels with LSPs for which it is the ingress at multiple levels. By analogy, it has become an intermediate LSR for concatenated LSPs corresponding to each label popped off where a corresponding label is also pushed onto the label stack.

To generalize:

- LSRs that push at least one more label onto a label stack than they pop off are ingress LSRs for LSPs at all levels corresponding to additional labels pushed.
- LSRs that pop at least one more label than they push are egress LSRs for LSPs corresponding to labels popped with no matching push.
- LSRs are intermediate LSRs in all LSPs for which they effectively perform a label swap.
- LSRs are transparent in all LSPs corresponding to labels that are unaffected by push, pop, and swap label manipulation instructions.

Note that this summary is a generalization. The simplicity of the forwarding function in MPLS depends on the fact that for any particular atomic forwarding decision, the decision is based entirely on the top-level label. Therefore, the NHLFE selection is based on the top-level label rather than the label stack in the simplified forwarding paradigm.

CHARACTERISTICS AND ASSOCIATED STATE

In addition to the forwarding information associated with an LSP, additional characteristics and state information may need to be maintained. Examples of these types of information include the following:

- QoS characteristics of the LSP, which are used to determine queue assignment and priority
- Information used to determine whether an LSP setup in progress can be merged with an existing LSP (if merging is supported)
- State of LSP setup, used to determine when the LSP may be used for forwarding data (in ordered control mode or when a loop has been detected)[14]

---

14. See Loops and Loop Mitigation, Detection, and Prevention in Chapter 6 for more information on loops.

Labeled Packets

This section describes the MPLS-specific components that make up a labeled packet.

LABEL

MPLS defines specific label formats for ATM and Frame Relay, and a generic label format intended for use with most other media.[15] ATM labels correspond to VPI/VCI numbers and may be as long as 24 bits. Frame Relay labels correspond to DLCI numbers and are either 10 or 23 bits long. The generic label is 20 bits long.

LABEL STACK

The label stack is a succession of labels in order (as viewed in network arrival order) from top to bottom. Operations on the label stack include the following:

- Pushing one or more labels onto the stack (adding labels to the beginning, or top, of the stack)
- Popping a label off the stack (removing it from the beginning, or top, of the stack)
- Swapping labels

The format of the label stack is described in the Encapsulation section in Chapter 6.

4.2 MPLS System Functions

This section describes the MPLS functions of distributing labels, merging of LSPs, manipulating the MPLS label stack, and selecting a route on which to forward a labeled packet.

Label Distribution

The distribution of labels—which includes allocation, distribution, and withdrawal of label and FEC bindings—is the mechanism on which MPLS most depends. It is the simple fact of agreeing on the meaning of a label

---

15. Specifically defined for use with PPP and Ethernet. See Encapsulation in Chapter 6.

that makes simplified forwarding on the basis of a fixed-length label possible. Protocols defined to aid in achieving this agreement between cooperating network devices are thus of paramount importance to the proper functioning of MPLS.

PIGGYBACK LABEL DISTRIBUTION

Labels may be transported in routing (and related) protocol messages. The attraction of this approach is that by piggybacking label assignments in the same protocol that is used to transport or define the associations (e.g., FECs) bound to those labels, the degree of consistency in assignment, validity, and use of those labels is increased. Consistency is made better by eliminating the use of additional messages that may lag behind and introduce a latency period in which, for instance, a route advertisement and its corresponding label(s) are inconsistent. Note that the latency resulting from a lag between route and label updates can be significant at very high packet transport speeds even if the delay is very small.

Examples of piggyback label distribution are discussed in Rekhter and Rosen (w.i.p.) and Awduche et al. (w.i.p.). See also the section entitled Label Distribution in Chapter 6.

GENERALIZED LABEL DISTRIBUTION

Labels may also be distributed using protocols designed for that specific purpose.[16] A label distribution protocol is useful under those circumstances in which no suitable piggyback protocol may be used. The attractions of this approach are as follows:

- The scope of a label distribution protocol is orthogonal to specific routing (and related) protocols.
- A label distribution protocol provides a direct means for determining the capabilities of LSR peers.
- The protocol is more likely to be semantically complete[17] relative to the label distribution process.

LDP (Andersson et al. 2001) is an example of a label distribution protocol.

---

16. See Label Distribution Protocol in Chapter 6.

17. Semantically complete in the sense that all required messages will easily be defined because there is no requirement to make the semantic operations fit into the framework of an essentially unrelated protocol.

MERGING GRANULARITY

Merging in MPLS is the process of grouping FECs that will result in an identical forwarding path within an MPLS domain into a single LSP. Without this process, multiple LSPs will be set up to follow the same routed path toward an MPLS egress that is common for FECs associated with each LSP. This is not an efficient use of labels. However, the egress for the MPLS domain for a set of FECs may wish to use a finer granularity for the LSPs arriving at its input interfaces (for example, ensuring that no two streams of traffic, which the egress will forward to different next hops, share the same input labels).

In general, the best combination of efficiency and purpose is achieved by allowing downstream LSRs to control the merging granularity.

If an LSR, which is not an egress, waits until it has received a mapping from its downstream peer(s) and simply adopts the level of granularity provided by the mappings it receives, the downstream peer controls the granularity of resulting LSPs. This is the recommended approach when using ordered control.[18]

If an LSR, which is not an egress, distributes labels upstream prior to having received label mappings from downstream, it may discover that the label mappings it subsequently receives are based on a different level of granularity. In this case, the LSR may have to do one of the following:

- Withdraw some or all of its label mappings and reissue mappings with a matching granularity.

- Merge streams associated with finer-granularity label mappings sent to upstream peers into a smaller set of coarser-granularity label mappings from downstream.

- Choose a subset of finer-granularity label mappings from downstream to splice with the smaller set of coarser-granularity label mappings sent upstream.[19]

An LSR operating in independent control mode that is merge capable may follow a policy that results in its typically sending slightly finer granularity

---

18. See Control Modes and, in particular, Ordered Control Mode, later in this chapter.
19. The MPLS architecture Internet Draft (Rosen, Viswanathan, and Callon 2000) warns that this action may only be performed when it is possible for the upstream LSR to determine that doing so will not result in the streams of traffic following a path other than the routed path; otherwise, a stable loop may be established.

mappings to upstream peers than it typically receives from its downstream peers. If it does this, it can then merge the streams received on the finer-granularity LSPs from upstream to send on to the coarser LSPs downstream.

An LSR operating in independent control mode that is not merge capable must either withdraw and reissue label mappings upstream to match the granularity used downstream or request matching-granularity label mappings from downstream.

Merging

Merging is an essential feature in getting MPLS to scale to at least as large as a typical routed network. With no merge capability whatever, LSPs must be established from each ingress point to each egress point (producing on the order of n^2 LSPs, where n is the number of LSRs serving as edge nodes).[20] With even partial merge capability, however, the number of LSPs required is substantially reduced (toward order n). With merge capability available and in use at every node, it is possible to set up multipoint-to-point LSPs such that only a single label is consumed per FEC at each LSR—including all egress LSRs.

Different levels of merge capability are defined so that LSRs can support at least partial merge capability even when full merge capability is hard to do given the switching hardware (as is the case with many ATM switches).

FRAME MERGE

Frame merge is the capability typical of standard routing and is a natural consequence of transport media that encapsulate an entire L3 packet inside an L2 frame. In this case, full merging occurs naturally and no action is required of the LSR. This is typically the case with non-ATM L2 technologies.

VC MERGE

VC merge is the name applied to any technique that, when used with an ATM switch, allows it to effectively perform frame merging. Typically, this requires queuing cells associated with a single ATM Adaptation Layer (AAL) frame (if they are not actually reassembled) until the last one has been

---

20. An MPLS *edge node* is a node that has a routing neighbor that is not an LSR, or has an interface to a network that does not support label encapsulation. It may also be referred to as a *label edge router* (LER).

received. Those cells are then transmitted in the same order in which they were received, while being careful not to interleave them with cells from any other AAL frame being transmitted on the same VC. Interleaving cells using different VCIs is permissible; however, cells associated with the same VCI on any input interface must be transmitted without interleaving with cells received on other input interfaces (or the same interface using a different VCI) that will be transmitted using the same VCI.

Interleaving cells from different input VPI/VCIs onto the same output VPI/VCI makes it impossible for the receiver of the interleaved cells (from at least two sources) to determine where the frame boundaries should be when reassembling the cells into a higher-layer frame. The end-of-frame markers from multiple frames are interleaved as well, which would cause the cells from part of one frame to be assembled with cells from part of another frame (from a different source VPI/VCI), producing a completely useless assembled frame. To successfully merge traffic at the VPI/VCI level, the first cell from one input VPI/VCI must not be sent on an output VPI/VCI until the last cell from another input VPI/VCI has been sent on that same output VPI/VCI.

VC merging therefore requires that cells from each input VPI/VCI to be merged be queued until the last cell from other merging input VPI/VCIs has been sent on the same output VPI/VCI. Figure 4.2 shows the difference between interleaving and VC merging input VPI/VCIs onto a single output VPI/VCI. Using the train analogy from earlier, it is easy to see that the cars associated with one train must not become attached to the engine for another train in the process of merging the two trains onto the same track.

VP MERGE

VP merge is the name applied to any technique that provides for mapping distinct VCI numbers on different virtual paths (VPs) at input interfaces to the same VP at an output interface. Because distinct VCIs are used in transmitting cells on an output interface, it is not possible to interleave cells from different input streams at the output interface.

Label Stack Manipulation

Figure 4.3 illustrates stack manipulations associated with the label swap, pop, and push operations described in this section.

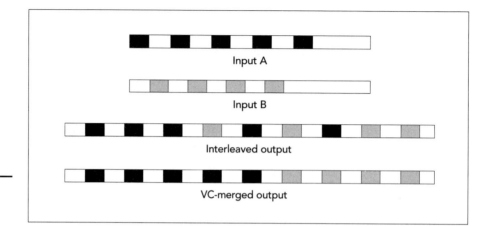

FIGURE 4.2

VC merging
avoiding cell
interleaving

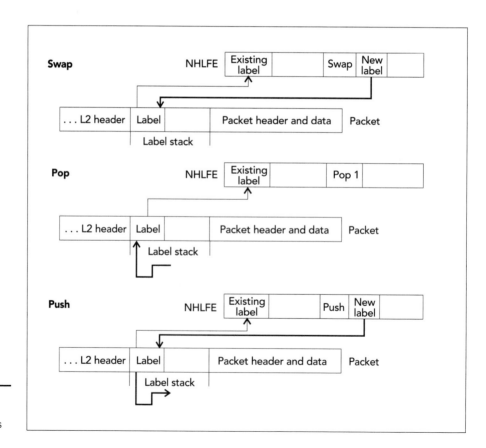

FIGURE 4.3

Label and
label stack
manipulations

LABEL SWAP

In a label swap, the label used to pick an ILM is swapped with a label provided as part of the swap label manipulation instruction in the NHLFE. The peer LSR associated with the next hop in the NHLFE distributed the new label to the local LSR at some point.

POP

In a pop operation, the label used to pick an ILM is removed from the packet, and the next label in the stack—if present—is put in its place. Each remaining label in the label stack is promoted one level (shifted left one word). If no label stack remains (the removed label's stack-entry bottom-of-stack bit is set), the packet is sent unlabeled on the interface indicated in the NHLFE.

PUSH

In a push operation, a new label from an NHLFE is inserted, existing labels in the label stack are demoted one level (shifted right one word), and a new stack entry is made for the newly added label. If no stack existed previously, the LSR creates one stack entry containing the new label.

Note that for each pop or push operation, additional actions may be required (such as setting the bottom-of-stack bit if this is the first label being pushed, copying the TTL value from the previous top-level label to the new top-level label, and so on).

Route Selection

Methods for selecting routes in an LSR are discussed in this section.

USING HOP-BY-HOP ROUTING

Hop-by-hop routing corresponds to normal routing. Each LSR is free to choose the next hop it will use in forwarding packets toward a destination (corresponding to an FEC), using its internal route computation.

USING EXPLICIT ROUTING

Explicit routing is the process used when an individual LSR[21] specifies a nonempty set of the hops to be used in an LSP. If all the hops are specified, it is a *strict explicit route*. Otherwise, it is a *loose explicit route*. The path used to get from one explicit hop to the next may be determined using hop-by-hop routing or may itself be specified as a strict or loose explicit route.[22] Based on this understanding of loose explicit routing, you should be able to see that "normal routing" is effectively a special case of loose explicit routing in which only the destination is specified.

4.3 MPLS Operating Modes

This section discusses several MPLS operating modes.

Label Allocation Modes

The label allocation mode refers to which of a given pair of LSRs will be allocating the labels that will be used on traffic sent from one to the other. For a given stream of data, the LSR that is required to interpret the label on packets in the stream received from the other LSR is the *downstream* LSR. The LSR that puts the label on packets in the stream that it sends to another LSR is the *upstream* LSR.

DOWNSTREAM LABEL ALLOCATION

Downstream label allocation is the only mode currently defined for MPLS. Using this approach allows for a minimal amount of label negotiation

---

21. Typically, this would be either an ingress or an egress LSR, although it is as easy to imagine a subset of all routers in a network being configured to dynamically establish explicit routes that include themselves as a hop. In this case, it would be useful if setting up explicit routes had been defined in both directions. Currently, both Jamoussi (w.i.p.) and Awduche et al. (w.i.p.) define mechanisms that may be used to establish explicit routes from ingress to egress.

22. The technique of using a new explicit route to define loose hops in an explicit-route LSP being set up is commonly referred to as *hierarchical explicit-route LSP setup*. If the intention is to use explicit routing at any level capable of recognizing what hops should be explicitly specified, the resulting LSP may be referred to as a *strict hierarchical explicit-route LSP setup*.

because the LSR that is required to interpret labels is responsible for assigning them.

UPSTREAM LABEL ALLOCATION

Upstream label allocation is not a supported mode in the current version of MPLS. The advantage associated with this label allocation mode is that switching hardware could realize significant gains from being able to use the same label on a number of different interfaces for multicast traffic.

Label Distribution Modes

This section describes MPLS modes specific to distributing MPLS labels.

DOWNSTREAM ON-DEMAND LABEL DISTRIBUTION

In downstream on-demand mode, label mappings are provided to an upstream LSR when requested. Because labels will not usually be requested unless needed for an NHLFE, this approach results in substantially less label-release traffic for unwanted labels when conservative label retention is in use and when the number of candidate interfaces that will not be used for a next hop is relatively large.

All LSRs must be able to provide labels when requested because (in the case where an LSR is not merge capable) the upstream LSR will need as many labels for LSPs going downstream as it has LSPs arriving at it from upstream. There is no standard way that a downstream LSR would know in advance how many labels to provide to an upstream peer; hence, the downstream LSR must be able to provide new labels as requested.

In addition, even an LSR that relies for the most part on downstream unsolicited label distribution will from time to time need to obtain a label that it released earlier. This is true because—whether the LSR uses conservative or liberal retention mode (described later)—the LSR may release labels it is unlikely to use given a particular routing topology. If the topology changes in a significant way (for instance, the routed path for some streams is reversed from what it was earlier), these labels will be suddenly and (possibly) unexpectedly needed. Thus, the basic capabilities associated with downstream on-demand distribution must be present regardless of the dominant mode used by an LSR.

DOWNSTREAM UNSOLICITED LABEL DISTRIBUTION

In downstream unsolicited mode, label mappings are provided to all peers for which the local LSR might be a next hop for a given FEC.[23] This would typically be done at least once during the lifetime of a peer relationship between adjacent LSRs.

Label Retention Modes

Label retention mode refers to the way in which an LSR treats label mappings it is not currently using. Note that the label retention mode may be particularly uninteresting when the downstream on-demand label distribution mode is in use.

CONSERVATIVE LABEL RETENTION

In the conservative label retention mode, any label mapping received from a peer LSR that is not used in an active NHLFE is released.

The advantage of this mode is that only labels that will be used given the existing topology are retained, reducing the amount of memory consumed in retaining labels. The potential cost is delay in obtaining new labels when a topology change occurs. When this mode is combined with downstream on-demand label distribution (as is most likely the case), the number of labels distributed from adjacent peers will be fewer as well.

LIBERAL LABEL RETENTION

In the liberal label retention mode, any label mapping that may ever be used as part of an active NHLFE is retained—up to and including all label mappings received.

The advantage of this mode is that should a topology change occur, the labels to use in the new topology are usually already in place. This advantage is realized at the price of storing labels that are not in use. For label-switching devices that have large numbers of ports, this memory cost can be very high because the likelihood that any particular label will be used to forward packets out of any particular port is, in general, inversely proportional to the total number of ports.

---

23. This would eliminate, for example, the LSR that is the next hop for the FEC associated with label mappings about to be sent.

INTERACTION BETWEEN LABEL DISTRIBUTION AND RETENTION MODES

The interaction between label distribution and retention is such that conservative retention is a more natural fit for downstream on-demand distribution, whereas liberal retention is a more natural fit for downstream unsolicited distribution. The reason is the need to send messages to release unused labels in both distribution modes and to specifically request labels in downstream on-demand distribution.

In the conservative retention mode, it does not make sense to get unsolicited labels because most of these will subsequently be released. For label-switching devices with many peers, the amount of message traffic associated with releasing unwanted labels (received as a result of downstream unsolicited distribution) after each routing change will typically be many times the number of messages required to request and receive labels using downstream on-demand distribution.

In the liberal retention mode, it does not make sense to use downstream on-demand distribution because of the need to specifically request labels for all FECs from all peers. If liberal retention is to be used, downstream unsolicited distribution mode effectively eliminates half of the message traffic otherwise required.

However, as implied earlier, when downstream on-demand distribution is used, it is arguable that liberal retention is also used, since all label mappings received from peers are retained. The spirit of liberal retention is to retain labels for all peers—at least one label from each peer and for each FEC. To achieve this using downstream on-demand distribution is clearly a suboptimal approach.

Control Modes

The distinction between the ordered and independent control modes is, in practice, likely to be a lot less than people have made it out to be in theory. With specific exceptions (for instance, traffic engineering tunnels, discussed later), choice of control mode is local rather than network wide. In addition, certain behaviors associated with a strict interpretation of control mode can result in pathological misbehavior within the network.

ORDERED CONTROL MODE

In ordered control mode, LSP setup is initiated at one point and propagates from there toward a termination point. In the case where LSP setup is initiated at an ingress, label requests are propagated all the way to an egress; label mappings are then returned until a label mapping arrives at the ingress. In the case where LSP setup is initiated at an egress, label mappings are propagated all the way to ingress points. A feature of ordered control is that an LSP is not completely set up until the associated messages have propagated from end to end—hence, data is not sent on the LSP until it is known to be loop free.

A severe disadvantage shows up in a purist implementation of ordered control mode in the following case. Assume that an LSR is the egress for a (potentially large) set of LSPs. This LSR now discovers a new peer that is downstream of it with respect to some or all of the set of LSPs for which the LSR is the current egress. If the local LSR simply adds the new LSR as an egress without somehow ascertaining that this LSR does not carry the LSP into a merge point upstream of the local LSR, it may introduce a loop into an LSP assumed to be loop free. If, on the other hand, it withdraws all label mappings upstream, it may produce a significant network outage and will result in a lot of LSP control activity, both of which might be unnecessary. For example, in the case where a downstream routing peer has just had MPLS enabled but is otherwise the same as it was previously, it is unlikely that forwarding will actually change.

One way to get around this problem is if the ordered-control LSR continues forwarding as before while it waits for label mappings (assuming it is getting downstream unsolicited label distributions) with a known (nonzero) hop count. In this way, the local LSR can continue to forward packets, using IP forwarding, to the routing peer to which it was forwarding previously.[24]

Waiting to receive a known hop count for a new LSP that is being established is one way for an intermediate LSR to use ordered control to force

---

24. If the new LSR peer is also a new routing peer, it must either be able to forward IP packets or to provide valid labels for forwarding labeled packets; otherwise, it should not advertise reachability for destinations to which it cannot forward packets. If a new routing peer is able to forward IP packets and is the new next hop for a set of IP packets, then those packets would be forwarded via that routing peer.

ordered control for a portion of the LSP. The fact that the LSP has been established for LSRs downstream is irrelevant if the LSP is not established to an ingress LSR, since no packets will be forwarded on that LSP until the LSP is established to an ingress LSR (by definition, packets are inserted on an LSP at ingress LSRs). Because this behavior prevents an LSP from being established between the local LSR and its upstream neighbors, the local LSR has succeeded in forcing ordered control on the LSP downstream and for at least the one hop to its upstream peers when one or more LSRs between that LSR and an egress are otherwise using independent control.

If an LSR continues to forward packets using IP (acting as the egress for a set of LSPs) even though it has discovered another LSR that should be the egress (for that set of LSPs), it is behaving as if it were using independent control—at least temporarily—in spite of the fact that it may be configured to use ordered control.

INDEPENDENT CONTROL MODE

Independent control mode is the mode in use when an LSR

- Has reason to believe that it will get label mappings from downstream peers for a specific FEC
- Distributes labels for that FEC to its upstream peers irrespective of whether it has received the expected label mappings from downstream

In this case, the LSR sending the label mapping includes a hop count that reflects the fact that it is not the egress and has not received label mappings (directly or indirectly) from an LSR that is. The special hop-count value of zero (unknown hop count) is used to indicate this case.

Upstream LSRs may or may not start to use the label mappings thus provided. Using the LSP is probably not advisable, because the LSR providing the label mapping may elect to discard packets (while waiting to receive label mappings from downstream peers), and the LSP is not proven to be loop free (until a label mapping is propagated from downstream with a known hop count).

In effect, if an LSP is never used until a label mapping for the LSP containing a known hop count is received at the ingress to the LSP, the network is behaving as if ordered control were in use for all LSRs along the given LSP.

Label Spaces

Label space refers to the scope of a label within a specific LSR and how this scope relates to an adjacent LSR peer. A label space is designated either per interface or per platform (Figure 4.4). Selection of the label space used for any interface is a configuration or implementation choice. In implementations, either per-interface or per-platform label space may be supported; however, no implementation is required to support both.[25]

The following general statements can be made about LSR implementations:

- ATM LSRs will most likely not support a per-platform label space. This is true because of the implications of assigning the same VPI/VCI meaning to all ATM interfaces.

- Support for the per-platform interface is easily achievable using generic MPLS labels (as is the case for PPP or LAN encapsulation, or label stacking).

- It is possible for per-platform label space to apply to some interfaces and not to others. Otherwise, the presence of a single ATM interface (or a diversity of interfaces) would preclude use of the per-platform label space.

- The interpretation of "per platform" is only required to be consistent for any implementation with respect to a single peer LSR instance. Thus, rules regarding interpretation of labels distributed to a single LSR peer instance do not necessarily apply to labels distributed to another peer instance, even when both peers are using the per-platform label space.[26]

A per-interface label space applies when the same label may be interpreted differently at a given interface than it would be at other interfaces, even when these interfaces are in common with the same LSR peer instance. This situation would be likely for ATM or Frame Relay interfaces of an LSR.

---

25. It is likely, however, that a specific configuration of an implementation (for example, one that includes both ATM and Ethernet interfaces) may make avoiding support for both label spaces difficult and possibly unreasonable.

26. In fact, as has been discussed on the MPLS mailing list, it is actually not correct for an LSR to accept labels from a peer to which it has not distributed those same labels—even if a simplistic interpretation of the meaning of per-platform label space would lead to this behavior. The reason for this is the implied level of trust associated with accepting labeled packets.

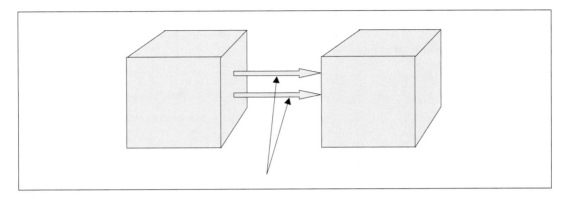

FIGURE 4.4

Per-platform label space. With per-platform labels, packets may be forwarded using either of these two links using the same labels. With per-interface labels, this is not guaranteed.

A per-platform label space applies when the same label will be interpreted the same way at least for all interfaces in common with a peer LSR. An LSR may be able to support multiple per-platform label spaces as long as it is able to ensure that it does not attempt to do so in a way that is visible to any peer LSR instance. In other words, an LSR can advertise two disjoint label spaces as "per-platform" to two different LSR peers and assign and interpret labels accordingly as long as the local LSR can be certain that they are distinct peers. An LSR may not be able to support multiple per-platform label spaces if it is not possible to determine which interfaces are in common with each peer LSR.

To understand use of the per-platform label space, it is necessary to understand the motivation for defining it. Interpretation of labels in the per-interface case means matching the incoming interface and the label to determine the outgoing interface, label, and so on. In theory, at least, the per-platform label space allows the implementation to perform a match based on the label alone. In practice, this may not be an acceptable behavior. For one thing, it allows labels received on an interface to direct labeled packets out the same interface (an exceptionally pathological behavior). For another, it allows an LSR to use labels (and associated resources) it was not intended to use.

Another possible motivation for use of a per-platform label space is to avoid the necessity of advertising multiple labels for interfaces in common between a pair of LSRs. In this case, however, it is only necessary that labels be shared for interfaces in common. In some implementation architectures, this can easily be done.

References

Andersson, Loa, Paul Doolan, Nancy Feldman, Andre Fredette, and Bob Thomas. 2001 (January). LDP specification, RFC 3036. Available at http://www.isi.edu/in-notes/rfc3036.txt.

Awduche, Daniel O., Lou Berger, Der-Hwa Gan, Tony Li, Vijay Srinivasan, and George Swallow. RSVP-TE: Extensions to RSVP for LSP tunnels; a work in progress.

IANA (Internet Assigned Numbers Authority). Undated a. Ether types. Available at http://www.isi.edu/in-notes/iana/assignments/ethernet-numbers.

IANA (Internet Assigned Numbers Authority). Undated b. Point-to-Point Protocol field assignments. Available at http://www.isi.edu/in-notes/iana/assignments/ppp-numbers.

Jamoussi, Bilel, ed. Constraint-based LSP setup using LDP; a work in progress.

Rekhter, Yakov, and Eric C. Rosen. 2000 (January). Carrying label information in BGP-4; a work in progress.

Rosen, Eric C., Yakov Rekhter, Daniel Tappan, Dino Farinacci, Guy Fedorkow, Tony Li, and Alex Conta. 2001 (January). MPLS label stack encoding. RFC 3032. Available at http://www.isi.edu/in-notes/rfc3032.txt.

Rosen, Eric C., Arun Viswanathan, and Ross Callon. 2001 (January). Multiprotocol Label Switching architecture. RFC 3031. Available at http://www.isi.edu/in-notes/rfc3031.txt.

5

Applicability

Everyone should do as they like, and if they don't, they should be made to.

•*paraphrased from 20,000 Quips and Quotes, Evan Esar (ed.)*

5.1 General

 MPLS applicability is largely an issue of trade-offs in differing deployment values and concerns. As discussed in the Requirements section of Chapter 3, deployment concerns affect the costs and benefits associated with MPLS.

MPLS may be applicable where it can be immediately—or very quickly—made ubiquitous in a network or in large sections of a network. This may be the case if the network is a green-field deployment,[1] the MPLS capability exists already in deployed routers or switches needing only to be turned on, or the MPLS capability is easily added (for example, by flash download or software upgrade) to deployed routers or switches.

Under circumstances in which MPLS capabilities exist in substantial contiguous portions of a network, MPLS may be applicable based on a comparison of collective benefit (in terms of reduced cost, relative insensitivity to volatile route change activity, use of tunneling, etc.) to core, or backbone, routing in the network with collective cost (in terms of additional interface complexity, memory usage, state maintenance, and protocol activity), particularly in edgeward LSRs.

---

1. The term *green field* is frequently used to indicate that compatibility with existing deployment is not an issue—usually because such a deployment does not exist.

The benefit of using MPLS is greatest in networks in which a fairly large fraction of all network components (particularly coreward switches) have essentially no layer 3 forwarding capability (potentially gaining some benefit from reduced complexity in the forwarding function). Irrespective of the relative complexity of MPLS versus IP forwarding, it is more complicated still to be required to forward both ways. It follows from this that the cost of MPLS equipment is least in networks with MPLS domains having a relatively thin edge (that is, edge switches that have L3 interfaces and MPLS interfaces but no hybrid interfaces).[2]

The cost-benefit ratio is made more favorable if the majority of MPLS switches are either frame or VC merge capable because this reduces the number of LSPs that each edgeward LSR needs to have information for (state, labels, etc.) relative to all other edgeward LSRs in a single MPLS domain. This results in a lower cost associated with edgeward LSR complexity for an MPLS domain of any given size, thus allowing for MPLS domains of larger sizes and, possibly, a higher proportion of exclusively label-switching network devices.

MPLS domains that have thin edges and are dominated by switches having little or no L3 forwarding capability are likely to be limited in size, however, by sensitivity to route changes in the network core, or backbone. This will be particularly true if routing is used exclusively to provide failover capabilities, because data may stop being forwarded in large portions of the network while routing stabilizes and loop-free LSPs are set up end to end after a routing transient. This may lead to unacceptable service outages.

Network sizes may also be effectively limited by the protocols used to piggyback label distribution, if such protocols are used. LSP setup may depend on use of a common signaling protocol in a common frame of reference (in order to reduce LSP setup complexity and the potential for invalid setup).[3]

---

2. Hybrid interfaces, in this context, are interfaces capable of sending and receiving both labeled and unlabeled packets. Note that such interfaces naturally exist in pairs because it does not make sense to send packets that cannot be received.

3. It certainly may turn out that there are exceptions to this rule as network engineers gain experience with use of various MPLS implementations. However, it would probably be ill advised to assume that vendors will immediately support LSP signaling translation directly from one label distribution mechanism (or protocol domain) to another, and that such implementations will interoperate correctly in a multivendor environment.

The protocol used to piggyback labels may have scaling limitations more restrictive than the scaling limitations existing for MPLS itself.

5.2 Encapsulation of Packets

A generic label stack encapsulation is defined specifically to be used in LAN and PPP networking equipment as a shim header between data-link-layer encapsulation (such as Ethernet or Token Ring) and network-layer encapsulation (specifically, IPv4). Specific encapsulations are defined with link-layer modifications for Frame Relay and ATM, as well, and additional encapsulations may be defined in the future. See Encapsulation in Chapter 6 for more detail on this subject.

MPLS encapsulation, in any medium so far defined, does not require the encapsulated data to start with an IPv4 encapsulation in every case, however. Two end points of any LSP—established for some purpose known to both—can use any encapsulation that may be appropriate on this LSP. In this sense, packets are effectively treated as if they were encapsulated in an outer IP header (represented, or abbreviated, by the MPLS shim header or—in ATM or Frame Relay—by the data-link header) in forwarding from the LSP ingress to the LSP egress. Of course, whatever encapsulation is used in lieu of IP must provide those IP functions required by the application.[4]

5.3 Signaling

Considerable debate exists regarding which signaling protocol is most appropriate under what circumstances. Table 5.1 lists alternative protocols and the applications for which they've been considered. The truth is that any of these protocols can be made to meet the needs of the application shown. However, certain considerations may have an impact on which of the signaling protocols would be selected in many cases.

---

4. For instance, the MPLS shim header does not contain sufficient information to reorder packets that may arrive out of order. Under most normal circumstances, this is not critical. However, some potential uses for MPLS may be highly sensitive to ordered delivery, and some implementations might not make this a priority because it is not a technical requirement of the protocol.

Table 5.1.   Signaling Alternatives and Applications

Alternative A	Alternative B	Application
LDP	RSVP-TE	Hop-by-hop routed LSP operation
CR-LDP	RSVP-TE	Traffic engineering LSP operation
CR-LDP	MPLS-BGP	Virtual private network LSP operation

LDP, Label Distribution Protocol; RSVP-TE, Reservation Protocol tunneling extensions; CR-LDP, Constraint-based Routing Label Distribution Protocol; MPLS-BGP, MPLS extensions for Border Gateway Protocol.

Hard-State versus Soft-State Protocols

As a background to further discussion, it is necessary to first understand the distinction between soft-state and hard-state protocols.

A *soft-state protocol* is one in which the failure to receive an update or refresh of state information causes the information to become out of date and be discarded. A soft-state protocol can operate fairly well in an environment in which delivery of update or refresh message events is not reliable. This is because nondelivery of a sufficient number of refresh messages will cause out-of-date state to be removed, and relatively frequent retransmission of refreshes will ensure that a missed message is eventually received. Refresh is required, and state information must be expunged at some point if it is not refreshed. The Reservation Protocol (RSVP) is often referred to as a soft-state protocol.

A *hard-state protocol* is one in which state information remains valid until explicitly changed. Proper operation of a hard-state protocol requires absolute reliability in delivery of message events because it must not be possible for events to be missed. Most protocols that are considered hard state are based on Transmission Control Protocol (TCP). For example, both Border Gateway Protocol (BGP) and Label Distribution Protocol (LDP) use TCP. TCP guarantees delivery of all messages sent during the duration of a connection; therefore, protocols based on TCP may rely on delivery of message events for as long as a connection exists and must assume that all state information is invalid once a connection no longer exists.

The boundary between soft- and hard-state protocols is not always clear-cut. For example, addition of reliability mechanisms to a soft-state protocol in effect makes the protocol a hard-state protocol. At the same time, circumstances that may result in failure to remove invalid state information in a hard-state protocol may require use of timers and other mechanisms in ways that are very similar to soft-state protocols. Based on these definitions of hard and soft state, it is not unreasonable to argue that TCP is a soft-state protocol because the connection state depends on refresh (in the form of Hello messages). In addition, many protocols that use TCP also implement either hello or keep-alive activity to ensure the integrity of the protocol engines.

LDP

The Label Distribution Protocol is based on TCP and is thus a hard-state protocol.

LDP was primarily designed—based on the original Tag Distribution Protocol (TDP) and Aggregate Route-based IP Switching (ARIS) signaling proposals—as a mechanism to be used in setting up LSPs for hop-by-hop routing. For this reason, the simplest use of LDP is to establish single links of LSPs at a time. This can be done using either downstream unsolicited or downstream on-demand label distribution and is compatible with either ordered or independent control. Either liberal or conservative label retention may be used at any LSR. However, certain combinations make more sense.

For example, having neighboring LSRs using downstream unsolicited distribution can result in a lot of label-release traffic if the local LSR is using conservative retention. Because only one interface (typically) is used to forward packets associated with a particular FEC, label mappings received for other interfaces would be released in conservative retention mode. Assuming that an LSR receives unsolicited label mappings for R route table entries it has from all of its peers and that it releases labels for each interface that is not used to forward packets to the next hop in a specific route table entry, an LSR having N interfaces will need to release on average

$$[(N{-}1) \times R] \, / \, N$$

labels for each interface. Therefore, the total number of Label Release messages sent by the local LSR would be

$$(N{-}1) \times R$$

In reality, however, not all neighboring LSRs will send Label Mapping messages for every route in the local LSR's route table. In particular, LSRs that show the local LSR as the next hop (in their own route table) for a particular route entry should not provide a label mapping to this LSR for that route entry. This will—in theory at least—reduce the number of Label Release messages required.

Similarly, having neighboring LSRs using downstream on-demand distribution can result in a lot of label-request traffic if the local LSR wants to use liberal retention and obtain labels for all of its interfaces. Therefore, the use of conservative retention implies the use of downstream on-demand distribution, and vice versa.

CR-LDP

Constraint-based Routing Label Distribution Protocol (CR-LDP) provides extensions to the base LDP for support of explicitly routing LSP setup requests and (potentially) reserving resources along the resulting LSP. The capability of specifying an explicit route to be used in LSP setup permits the network operator or network management system to establish LSPs that are constrained by considerations other than the necessity of following a routed path strictly. The ability to associate resources with such an LSP allows traffic to be channeled across the network routing infrastructure to provide traffic engineering or virtual private networking services. Explicitly routing LSPs is useful as well in assuring that an LSP is continuous over the specified list of LSRs.

Explicitly routed LSPs may be used to establish a VPN service that is independent of routing protocols in the providing network. This is very useful, for example, if it is not desirable to require an edge router on customer premises. CR-LDP may be used to provide this service by establishing explicitly routed tunnels to carry VPN traffic.

RSVP-TE

RSVP-TE provides extensions of the base RSVP for support of explicitly routed LSP setup requests. These extensions are specifically defined to support LSP tunnels. RSVP itself defines mechanisms for support of allocation of network resources to the paths defined by protocol activity. The capability of specifying an explicit route to be used in LSP setup permits the network operator or network management system to establish LSPs that are not restricted to following a routed path strictly. The ability to associate resources with such an LSP allows traffic to be channeled across the network routing infrastructure to provide traffic engineering or virtual private networking services.

RSVP-TE (as currently defined) is a soft-state protocol. Because of existing scaling limitations of RSVP-TE, it may not currently be as suitable a candidate for support of VPNs as are some of the available alternatives (for example, MPLS-BGP or CR-LDP). Support for VPNs requires numbers of LSPs in proportion to the number of distinct VPNs being supported and (depending on the approach alternatives being used) in proportion to the square of the number of end points for each VPN.

RSVP-TE also allows for piggybacking MPLS labels in basic RSVP operation by excluding the Explicit Route object in protocol messages. In this usage, the extensions provide a simple added value by allowing MPLS labels to be bound to the RSVP reservations as they are made.

RSVP-TE may also be used to set up best-effort routed paths (in lieu of an explicit label distribution protocol) by setting reservation parameters such that no resources are committed for associated LSPs. Although this suggested approach is a proof of the concept that some label distribution needs may be met using the RSVP extensions, it does not seem likely that anyone will use RSVP-TE in this way.[5]

Explicitly routed LSPs may be used to establish a VPN service that is independent of routing protocols in the providing network. This is very useful, for example, if it is not desirable to require an edge router on customer premises. As was the case with CR-LDP, RSVP-TE may also be used to provide this service by establishing explicitly routed tunnels to carry VPN traffic.

---

5. This suggestion actually points out a weakness in arguments that claimed RSVP scalability issues were an exaggeration, because it is readily apparent that RSVP-TE minus explicit routes and resource reservations is not equal to LDP in terms of protocol complexity, reliability, scalability, and other factors.

MPLS-BGP

MPLS extensions for BGP (MPLS-BGP) (Rekhter and Rosen w.i.p.) are defined for carrying labels in BGP version 4 (Rekhter and Li 1995). Using these extensions, BGP speakers[6] can distribute labels to other border routers directly in Update messages (via piggyback label distribution). Using this approach helps to ensure that distributed labels and routing information are consistent and reduces the overhead of processing control messages.

Within a network that uses BGP routers as border routers to other networks, it is common to have non-BGP speakers connecting these border routers. Where two BGP routers are not immediately adjacent, it is necessary to establish an LSP between these routers using some other mechanism for label distribution. Similarly, it is important that these two BGP routers be connected by a pair of continuous LSPs.

In Figure 5.1, it is not possible to establish an LSP between border routers B1 and B3. Border router B1 is not always directly able to tell that this is the case because an attempt to establish an LSP to the router address of B3 will succeed. LSR L1 will determine that it is the egress for the requested LSP (regardless of whether it selects router R1 or R2, its next hop is not an LSR and therefore it is the egress for the specified FEC) and will return a label mapping to B1. B1 may, at this point, be able to compare a hop count present in the Label Mapping message with its own knowledge of the local topology (perhaps derived from an intradomain routing protocol) and realize that the LSP thus successfully established cannot be continuous to B3. However, this might not be possible in a more complex topology, and there is no guarantee that B1 will perform this comparison.

Suppose that B3 similarly establishes an LSP to L2 for an FEC associated with B1. At this point, if the border routers exchange Update messages containing labels, one of two things will happen to the resulting labeled traffic between these two border routers (taking labeled packets going from B1 toward B3 as an example):

---

6. In the Border Gateway Protocol, routers that participate in routing protocol exchanges are referred to as *BGP speakers*. This includes border routers and route reflectors.

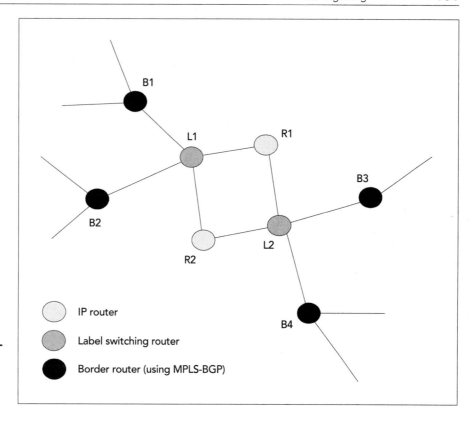

FIGURE 5.1

Effect of non-
continuous
LSPs between
BGP peers

1. Labeled packets arriving at L1 from B1 will be dropped.

2. Labeled packets arriving at L1 from B1 will be forwarded using IP
   routing.

The first alternative is more likely. The labels distributed using MPLS-BGP
are either swapped with existing labels at B1 (if labeled already) or pushed
onto a new label stack (if B1 is the ingress to a corresponding LSP), and
then a label for the LSP to B3 is pushed onto the label stack as well. At L1—
because it is the egress for the LSP to B3—the top label is popped and the
packet would normally be forwarded via IP routing to B3. However, in this
case, the label removed was not the bottom of the stack. Because L1 is
expecting the label associated with B3 to be the bottom of the label stack,
it might simply treat the fact that the label is not the bottom of the stack as
an error condition and drop the packet. Alternatively, it might keep popping the label stack until it has removed the last label and then forward the
packet as an IP packet.

According to discussions among the MPLS working group members, the second option is not always predictably useful. There are cases in which stripping off more than the expected number of labels would result in incorrect or impossible forwarding of packets, and it is not always possible to predict (a priori) when this will not be true. For this reason, the likely (at least default) behavior will be to drop packets in this case.

One might think that B1 could infer the existence of a continuous LSP to B3 from the existence of an LSP from B3. If this were the case, then each border router could decide which labels it might safely use based on the fact that it received them over an LSP. However, there are two problems with this approach:

1. Successful setup of an LSP from B3 to B1 does not necessarily ensure that a reciprocal continuous LSP was equally successful.

2. It is not necessarily possible to determine that an incoming LSP is continuous.

To illustrate the second observation, consider the case in which border router B1 attempts to set up an LSP to border router B3. This LSP terminates at LSR L1. LSR L2, however, has a route in its route table for B3 and establishes an LSP, on its own behalf, to B3. BGP Update messages forwarded on the LSP from B1 to L1 and IP-forwarded to L2 are then inserted into the LSP from L2 to B3, thus arriving on an LSP at B3. Hence—as the protocol is currently defined—it is not necessarily possible to determine that an existing LSP is continuous between two border routers.

One way that two BGP peers may be able to determine that continuous LSPs exist between them is via configuration. That is, the option to use MPLS-BGP is configured at B1 and B3 relative to each other based on prior knowledge that such LSPs will exist. Another approach is to establish the LSP using an explicit route including at least the desired BGP-speaking peer with which an LSP is desired.

MPLS-BGP may also be used in establishing a VPN service based on BGP routing. How this is done is defined in RFC 2547 (Rosen and Rekhter 1999). The scheme defined is primarily a flat (nonhierarchical) approach and requires special capabilities in BGP-speaking routers in a service provider network, specifically:

- The ability to maintain multiple separate route tables (on a per-VPN basis) in provider edge devices

- Support for a new address family for the address families supported in each VPN (currently, only VPN-IPv4 is defined) at each service provider BGP router.

This use of MPLS-BGP is also discussed in the section Piggyback Label Distribution Using BGP in Chapter 6.

References

Andersson, Loa, Paul Doolan, Nancy Feldman, Andre Fredette, and Bob Thomas. 2001 (January). LDP specification. RFC 3036. Available at http://www.isi.edu/in-notes/rfc3036.txt.

Ash, Jerry, Muckai Girish, Eric Gray, Bilel Jamoussi, and Gregory Wright. Applicability statement for CR-LDP, version 1; a work in progress.

Awduche, Daniel O., Lou Berger, Der-Hwa Gan, Tony Li, Vijay Srinivasan, and George Swallow. RSVP-TE: Extensions to RSVP for LSP tunnels; a work in progress.

Awduche, Daniel O., Alan Hannan, and Xipeng Xiao. Applicability statement for extensions to RSVP for LSP-tunnels; a work in progress.

Braden, Bob, Lixia Zhang, Steve Berson, Shai Herzog, and Sugih Jamin. 1997 (September). Resource ReSerVation Protocol (RSVP)—version 1 functional specification. RFC 2205. Available at http://www.isi.edu/in-notes/rfc2205.txt.

Jamoussi, Bilel, ed. Constraint-based LSP setup using LDP; a work in progress.

Rekhter, Yakov, and Tony Li. 1995 (March). A Border Gateway Protocol 4 (BGP-4). RFC 1771. Available at http://www.isi.edu/in-notes/rfc1771.txt.

Rekhter, Yakov, and Eric C. Rosen. Carrying label information in BGP-4, version 4; a work in progress.

Rosen, Eric C., and Yakov Rekhter. 1999 (March). BGP/MPLS VPNs. RFC 2547. Available at http://www.isi.edu/in-notes/rfc2547.txt.

Thomas, Bob, and Eric Gray. 2000 (August). LDP applicability. Available at http://www.isi.edu/in-notes/rfc3037.txt.

Part II

DETAILS OF THE STANDARD

6

IMPLEMENTATION ALTERNATIVES

6.1 Topology versus Flow

 As discussed in Chapter 2, many early proposals were either based on or included provisions for establishing some form of virtual circuit or path based on detection of a demand for such a circuit or path. As a class (including Ipsilon's IP-switching protocol, IFMP, and the ATM Forum's MPOA), these approaches are often referred to as *flow based*. Common to these approaches is the notion of tracking packet flows based on some combination of key packet header fields (for example, source and destination IP addresses or TCP port numbers, or both) and setting up a circuit to handle flows detected as a result of this tracking process.

ARIS and Cisco's tag-switching proposals, among others, have been referred to as *topology based*, primarily because topology—as determined from IP routing in particular—is used to drive the circuit setup process.

The key distinction between the two approaches lies in the answers to these questions: When does it make sense to set up an LSP (and consume associated resources), and how much tolerance is there for delay in determining that such an LSP is needed?

For best-effort forwarding of IP datagrams, resource consumption is limited to the labels used in setting up an LSP. There are no specific per-LSP queuing requirements. Where merging is used, the number of labels consumed at each LSR is of the same order as the number of routes known to the LSR. Hence, assuming there is some benefit in setting up best-effort LSPs for forwarding of IP datagrams,[1] there is little reason not to set up all required LSPs at once—with the qualification that LSPs be set up using the same granularity as is present in an LSR's routing table entries. Typically, such LSPs would be established using either LDP or MPLS-BGP.[2]

Where resources (queuing and buffering resources, for example) are going to be committed to an LSP, however, some mechanism is needed to determine when these resources are required. The flow-detection approaches proposed earlier have taken a new course, and current schemes depend on explicit signaling of the resource requirements to be associated with an LSP. The signaling approaches currently available for doing this are CR-LDP and RSVP-TE.[3]

Traffic engineering is—in its own way—a variation of previous flow-based approaches.[4] Previous flow-based approaches were concerned about bypassing the bottlenecks created by the process of making a routing decision at each router. Traffic engineering is concerned about bypassing bottlenecks created by the routing paradigm, that is, the determination of a single best route that leads to overutilization of some links and underutilization of others.

6.2 Tunneling

Probably the most important aspect of MPLS is the use of LSPs as tunnels. Tunneling of various types of data packets, including IP datagrams, is a fairly well-known technical approach to solving problems such as transport of non-IP packets, privacy, addressing, scalability of routing, mobility, and other data networking challenges.

---

1. See the discussion relative to wire-speed routing in Chapter 3.
2. See Andersson et al. (2001) and Rekhter and Rosen (w.i.p.).
3. See Jamoussi (w.i.p.) and Awduche et al. (w.i.p.).
4. See Awduche et al. (1999).

IP tunneling involves adding either an entire IP header or a fraction of an IP header[5] to the existing datagram. Using labels as the equivalent of a local abbreviation for an IP header allows tunneling at a cost of 4 bytes for each additional level of tunneling or encapsulation.

In addition to the relatively low impact on packet size (or reduction in available space for data transport), encapsulation and de-encapsulation is much simpler than other tunneling methods. New labels are simply pushed onto the label stack to encapsulate and popped off the label stack to de-encapsulate. There is no requirement to recompute an IP header checksum when encapsulating or de-encapsulating LSP tunneled packets.

This section discusses two types of LSP tunnels: peer-to-peer and explicit-route tunnels.

Peer-to-Peer Tunnels

Packets may be tunneled from one peer to another using a number of approaches. This section compares three approaches: IP in IP, minimal IP encapsulation, and MPLS.

ENCAPSULATION

As implied earlier, one way to create peer-to-peer tunnels is to use IP-in-IP encapsulation (Perkins 1996a). Using this approach adds a minimum of 20 bytes to the size of the IP packet (or reduces the maximum payload capacity by at least 20 bytes). Another option is to use minimal IP encapsulation (Perkins 1996b). Figure 6.1 compares these two approaches for encapsulating IP packets with analogous encapsulation using MPLS.

Using IP-in-IP encapsulation is directly comparable in that each new level of encapsulation is effectively pushed onto the packet. The previous IP header becomes part of the IP data in the resulting IP packet. De-encapsulation is analogous to popping an MPLS label in that the existing IP header is

---

5. See RFC 2004 (Perkins 1996b) for a minimal encapsulation approach. This approach applies to IP-in-IP encapsulation (RFC 2003; Perkins 1996a). The minimal encapsulation adds between 8 and 12 bytes for each new header. Another mechanism for tunneling IP packets is via use of either loose or strict source-routing IP options.

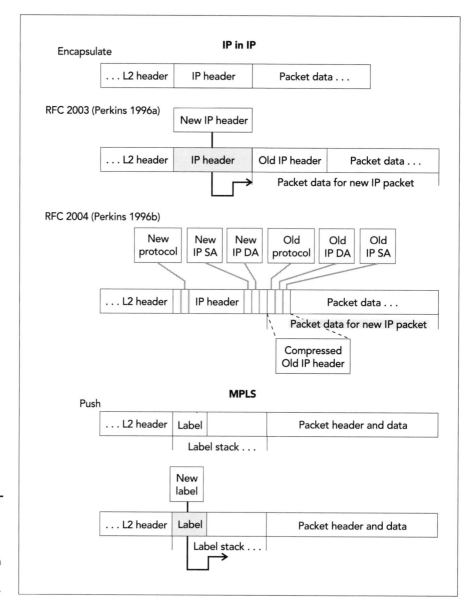

FIGURE 6.1

Comparison of tunneling encapsulation approaches. DA, destination address; SA, source address.

removed and the beginning of the IP data becomes the beginning of the new header. A key distinction is that each new IP header added is a full IP header, consisting of at least 20 bytes of data. When MPLS is used, only 4 bytes of additional data are added to the IP packet for each level of encapsulation.

Using minimal IP encapsulation results in reduced packet space overhead because this approach only adds either 8 or 12 bytes (depending on whether the source is also the encapsulation point)[6] rather than the 20 bytes added by IP in IP. This approach is fundamentally different from MPLS encapsulation in that only a portion of the existing IP header is "pushed" onto the front of the packet data (becoming, as with IP in IP, part of the packet data for the new packet). If this approach is used multiple times, successive IP protocol, source, and destination addresses are similarly pushed onto the head of the packet data (after the current IP header) while new values are written into the existing IP header. With this approach, the IP header checksum must be recomputed each time the packet is encapsulated or de-encapsulated.

Using MPLS to encapsulate an IP packet for tunneling is a slightly different process depending on whether or not the IP packet is already labeled. If the packet is already labeled (Figure 6.1 shows this case), the only action required is to push the new label onto the head of the label stack— between the L2 and L3 headers—and to insert the value associated with this label in the L2 header (for ATM and Frame Relay, it is also necessary to insert the value associated with this label). If the packet is not labeled, then a label stack is created by adding a generic label (Figure 6.2) between the L2 and L3 headers (with the bottom-of-stack bit set), and an L2 header is used that reflects that it encapsulates a labeled packet.

In each approach, de-encapsulation is done by reversing the encapsulation process. For example, in MPLS labeled tunnels, at the egress of the tunnel LSP (the tunnel destination), the label at the head of the label stack (the top label) is removed. If it was the last label, the following L3 header is used to

---

6. See Figure 6.1. The previous source IP address (Old IP SA) is added to a compressed representation of the previous IP header if it is different from the source address that would be added in encapsulating the packet. Because this form of encapsulation is more likely to be used by a gateway or proxy device, it is unlikely that the address will be the same. If the source IP address is the same, then the compressed header can be only 8 bytes long, since the source IP address can be omitted.

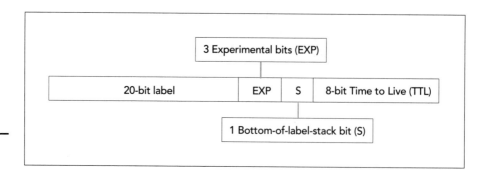

FIGURE 6.2

MPLS generic
label format

route the remaining packet. Otherwise, a lookup may be performed using
the next label in the stack, and the LSR acts on the basis of this lookup.[7]

TUNNEL ESTABLISHMENT

Generally, tunnels are set up between two systems to serve some purpose.
Consequently, as a result of configuration, communication between higher-
level applications, and so forth, the tunnel end points are aware of addresses
for each other that may be used in tunneling. Moreover, in the two IP tunneling examples, the IP protocol number tells the recipient of a tunneled
packet that the data portion of the packet starts with another IP header.[8]

MPLS uses mechanisms at two levels to allow a recipient to determine that
label encapsulation is in use. At the data-link layer, either explicit protocol
discriminators in the L2 header (Ethernet and PPP)[9] or implicit discrimina-
tion based on use of DLCI or VPI/VCI values associated with negotiated
labels is used to indicate that the packet contains an MPLS shim header.
Within the shim header, the value of the S (bottom-of-stack) bit allows the
recipient of a labeled packet to determine whether there are additional
labels in the stack or whether an L3 header follows the current label.[10]
Because it is possible for a recipient to determine that a packet has been
tunneled in each of these cases, it is not necessary for the receiving end of a

7. For the sake of simplicity, penultimate hop pop (PHP) and certain other variations are
   omitted in discussions in this section.

8. For IP in IP (Perkins 1996a), the IP protocol number is 4 (IP-encapsulated IP). For minimal encapsulation (Perkins 1996b), the IP protocol number is 55 (IP mobility).

9. See the Forwarding Module subsection of MPLS System Components in Chapter 4 for details.

10. Again, for simplicity, the possibility that the data following the label at the bottom of the
    label stack is not preceded directly by an L3 header is not discussed here.

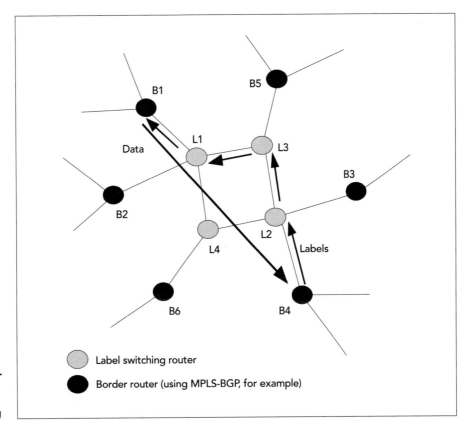

FIGURE 6.3

Negotiation of
stacked labels
in LSP tunneling

tunnel to have prior knowledge that a specific set of packets it receives are being tunneled. This greatly simplifies the setup process because it allows each end of an IP tunnel to unilaterally tunnel packets to the receiving end.[11]

In MPLS, tunnel setup is more reliable than in IP because of the need to use some mechanism to negotiate labels—particularly when labels are stacked to form LSP tunnels.

Figure 6.3 shows a set of LSRs across which an LSP tunnel will be established. In this figure, B1 establishes an LSP to B4 using (for example) LDP. The following steps occur (not necessarily in order):

---

11. This assumes that it is known in advance that the receiving end will "do the right thing" when it receives a tunneled packet. In real-world applications, it will be discovered fairly quickly if this is not true.

- B1 receives a label from L1 (for the FEC associated with B4).

- L1 similarly receives a label from L3.

- L3 receives a label from L2.

- L2 receives a label from B4.

A reciprocal LSP may be set up in the reverse direction using a similar set of steps. B4 now sends a label to B1 (possibly using MPLS-BGP). Because of the intervening LSRs in the LSP from B1 to B4, however, this label must be tunneled from B1 to B4. This is done as follows (in the order shown):

- B1 receives a packet that it will forward to B4.

- B1 puts the label received from B4 at the head of the label stack by swapping the existing label for the label for B4 or by pushing the label for B4 onto the label stack.

- B1 pushes the label for L1 onto the label stack and forwards the packet to L1.

- L1 swaps this label for the label received from L3 and forwards to L3.

- L3 swaps this label for the label received from L2 and forwards to L2.

- L2 swaps this label for the label received from B4 and forwards to B4.

- B4 recognizes that it is the destination from the label.

- B4 recognizes that the label is not the bottom of the stack.

- B4 pops the top label off the stack and uses the next label to switch the packet.

There are a few things to notice about this procedure. First, the label that B1 received from B4 cannot be used unless it is tunneled to B4. This label has no meaning to L1. Second, packets using this label should be tunneled using an LSP because there is no standard way to recognize that a tunnel of any other sort is carrying labeled packets. Finally, the labels received from B4 (by either L2 or B1) may be implicit Null labels, in which case a corresponding label is popped from the stack prior to forwarding the packet to B4 either directly or indirectly (via an LSP tunnel).

Explicit-Route Tunnels

Packets may also be effectively tunneled using explicit routing—for example, by using IP loose or strict source-routing options[12] or by using an explicitly routed LSP. This approach typically results in flat (as opposed to hierarchical) tunneling since the route a packet traverses is the result of a single level of encapsulation of a variable length rather than of successive levels of encapsulation between tunnel end points.

ENCAPSULATION

Figure 6.4 depicts the formats for an IP packet and loose or strict source-routing options. In routing a packet using either of these source-routing options, the packet is forwarded based on the current IP destination address. On arriving at the router with this address, the address pointed to by the option pointer/offset value is replaced by the source IP address the router would use if it were originating the packet, the pointer value is incremented by 4 (so that it now points to the next IPv4 address), and the destination IP address in the IP header is replaced by the IP address that is now pointed to. The distinction between the loose and strict source-routing options is that when using the latter, the packet is not forwarded if it is not directly reachable at this point.

One concern with using IP options in general is that their existence in an IP packet usually results in the packet's being processed in the "slow path." That is, packets using IP options are forwarded for processing to the control processor.

MPLS encapsulation for explicit, or source, routed label switching is as shown in Figure 6.1. A label is pushed onto the label stack (creating the label stack if necessary) on entry into the explicitly routed tunnel, and a label is popped off the stack on exit from the explicitly routed tunnel. No processing is required to be performed on the IP header during the forwarding process.

---

12. IP options 3 (131) and 9 (137), respectively, defined in RFC 791 (Postel 1981). The value actually used includes the high-order bit set (for copy on fragmenting).

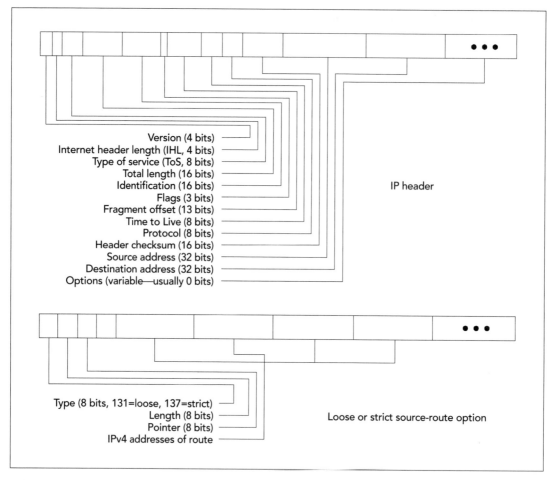

FIGURE 6.4

Source-routing IP option encapsulation

ESTABLISHING AN EXPLICIT-ROUTE TUNNEL

Using source-routing IP options requires no action in establishing a tunnel beyond configuring (or possibly computing) the route to be used at the source.

Using MPLS for explicit routing requires signaling an LSP setup along a specified loose or strict explicit route. The signaling approaches currently defined to allow this are CR-LDP and RSVP-TE.[13] This signaling process binds labels to the given route, eliminating the need to determine routing during the forwarding process.

6.3 Encapsulation

This section describes MPLS encapsulation both in terms of the aspects specific to individual media and the MPLS shim header.

Media Specifics

MPLS currently specifies media-specific behavior for ATM, Frame Relay, PPP, and Ethernet. These specifics are described in this section.

ATM

Figure 6.5 shows the preferred encapsulation of MPLS packets over ATM. It is possible to omit the label stack within the AAL5 protocol data unit (PDU) if it is known in advance that no MPLS packets will be carried with more than one label in the stack on a given ATM virtual circuit. If it is not possible to know this, then the AAL5 PDU must include a label stack even if there is only one entry (corresponding to the VPI/VCI used in the ATM virtual circuit). If a label stack is included, the first label in the stack is a generic label corresponding to the VPI/VCI used in the ATM layer header. Experimental (EXP), Time to Live (TTL), and bottom-of-stack (S) field values are significant, but the label field must be set to zero and ignored by the PDU recipient. The AAL5 PDU is then segmented and transmitted in 53-byte cells having the VPI/VCI values associated with a given LSP.

FRAME RELAY

Frame Relay encapsulation includes a generic label corresponding to the DLCI used in the Frame Relay L2 encapsulation. EXP, TTL, and S field values are significant, but the label field is meaningless (it is not used either in forwarding or as a key to determine new label or DLCI values in transiting from one Frame Relay switch to another).

---

13. See Jamoussi (w.i.p.) and Awduche et al. (w.i.p.).

FIGURE 6.5

ATM encapsu-
lation of MPLS
labeled pack-
ets. AAL5, ATM
Adaptation
Layer 5; CPCS,
Common Part
Convergence
Sublayer; PDU,
protocol data
unit.

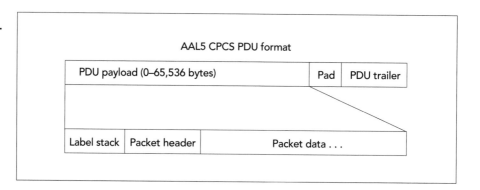

FIGURE 6.6

Frame Relay
encapsulation
of MPLS
labeled packets

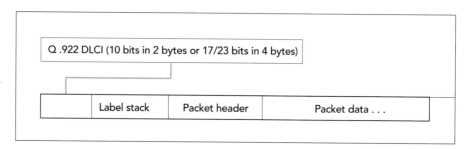

FIGURE 6.7

PPP encapsula-
tion of MPLS
labeled packets

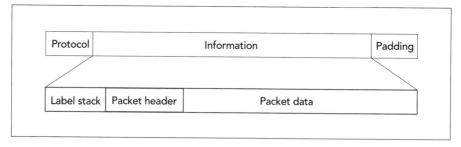

As shown in Figure 6.6, the label stack follows immediately after the Q.922
addressing header (which is either 2 or 4 bytes long, depending on whether
the DLCI is 10 or 23 bits long).

PPP AND POS

Figure 6.7 illustrates how MPLS labeled packets are encapsulated using the
Point-to-Point protocol. The Protocol field is assigned a value of 0×281 for
unicast MPLS packets and 0×283 for multicast MPLS packets.

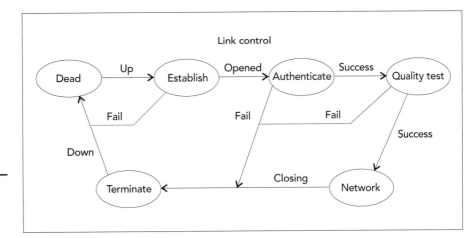

FIGURE 6.8

MPLS (Network) Control Protocol for PPP (MPLSCP)

Figure 6.8 shows the phases used in MPLS over PPP link and network control protocols. PPP links start in a Link Dead state with the link not yet ready. On detecting that the link is ready, Link Control Protocol (LCP)[14] goes into link establishment operation, sending configuration information between the two end points of the point-to-point link. If authentication is requested in the exchange of configuration information, LCP performs authentication. Similarly, if quality monitoring[15] was requested during link establishment, the link controller should ascertain that link quality is satisfactory by performing a quality test. Once the link is established and applicable authentication and quality testing is completed, the link controller enters the Network phase.

All MPLS Control Protocol (MPLSCP) messages are singly incorporated in the Information field of PPP encapsulation with the Protocol field set to $0\times 8281_{16}$. Once the LCP has reached the Network phase, each peer must send and receive at least one Configuration Request and Configuration Acknowledge before entering the opened state. After MPLSCP is in the open state, labeled packets may be sent on the PPP link.

ETHERNET

Figure 6.9 shows a breakdown of the IEEE 802.3/Ethernet encapsulation of an MPLS packet. The reserved Ethernet numbers 0x8847 (unicast) and

---

14. See RFC 1661 (Simpson 1994).

15. See RFC 1989 (Simpson 1996).

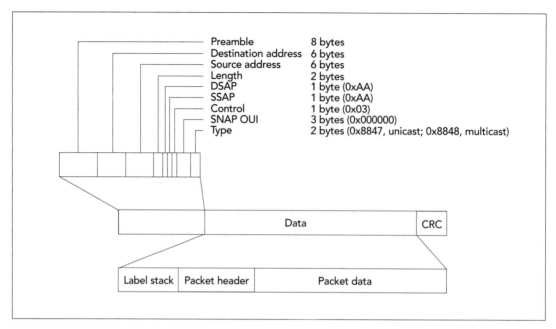

Preamble	8 bytes
Destination address	6 bytes
Source address	6 bytes
Length	2 bytes
DSAP	1 byte (0xAA)
SSAP	1 byte (0xAA)
Control	1 byte (0x03)
SNAP OUI	3 bytes (0x000000)
Type	2 bytes (0x8847, unicast; 0x8848, multicast)

Data | CRC

Label stack | Packet header | Packet data

FIGURE 6.9

Ethernet encapsulation of MPLS labeled packets

0×8848 (multicast) are used to distinguish MPLS encapsulated packets from other types of packets that might be received on an Ethernet interface (for example, IP packets, IP-in-IP tunneled packets).

Unlike PPP, IEEE 802.3/Ethernet does not involve any setup, other than signaling to establish valid labels, before MPLS encapsulated packets can be forwarded.

MPLS Shim

The format for an MPLS generic label is shown in Figure 6.2. It consists of a 20-bit label, a 3-bit field (currently reserved for experimental use), a bottom-of-stack bit, and an 8-bit TTL field. The top-level label entry contains the current value for TTL, which is copied, after decrementing, into the TTL field of any new label that may be in place as a result of a push or pop operation. The S bit (bottom-of-stack) is set when the current label is the last label in the stack, indicating that no further labels exist in the shim header.

For ATM and Frame Relay, the actual label value is carried in the appropriate L2 header, and the label field in the top-level label is meaningless.

The label stack consists of consecutive 32-bit label encodings, in order from the current top-level label to the bottom of the stack. The last label in the label stack can be found by looking at the S bit in each 32-bit label encoding.

6.4 Label Distribution

Piggyback Label Distribution Using BGP

BGP can carry labels in an Update message, in association with corresponding Network Layer Reachability Information (NLRI), using the format defined in MPLS-BGP (Rekhter and Rosen 2000) and shown in Figure 6.10. The approach is based on BGP multiprotocol extensions defined in RFC 2283 (Bates et al. 1998) and uses a new Subsequent Address Family Identifier (SAFI) code, namely, 4. The extensions define optional, nontransitive path attributes to carry both NLRI advertisements and withdrawals. Use of optional, nontransitive path attributes allows compatibility with standard BGP speakers as defined in RFC 1771 (Rekhter and Li 1995).

BGP Update messages defined in RFC 1771 carry a variable-length list of withdrawn routes, a variable-length list of path attributes, and up to one route advertisement. Using the path attributes defined in RFC 2283 allows advertisement of several routes in a single Update message and supports address families defined in RFC 1700 (Reynolds and Postel 1994) as qualified (unicast, multicast, and both) by SAFI values defined in RFC 2283. MPLS-BGP defines a new SAFI value and the format used to include MPLS labels.

As shown in Figure 6.10, labels are distributed via multiprotocol reachability path attributes and withdrawn via multiprotocol unreachability path attributes. Routes may be advertised using additional multiprotocol reachability attributes as well as by using the Update message NLRI field. The same route may be advertised both with and without labels, and different routes may be advertised for the same destination prefix as long as the labels for each such route are distinguishable.

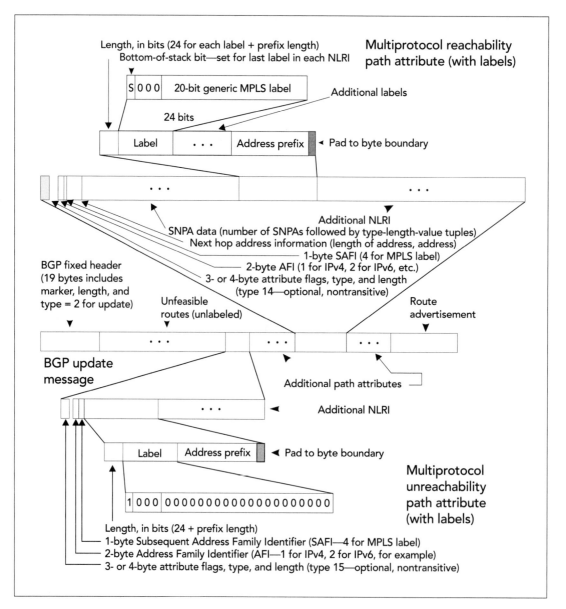

Length, in bits (24 for each label + prefix length)
Bottom-of-stack bit—set for last label in each NLRI

Multiprotocol reachability path attribute (with labels)

S 0 0 0 | 20-bit generic MPLS label

Additional labels

24 bits

Label . . . Address prefix ◄ Pad to byte boundary

. . . . . .

Additional NLRI
SNPA data (number of SNPAs followed by type-length-value tuples)
Next hop address information (length of address, address)
1-byte SAFI (4 for MPLS label)
2-byte AFI (1 for IPv4, 2 for IPv6, etc.)
3- or 4-byte attribute flags, type, and length
(type 14—optional, nontransitive)

BGP fixed header
(19 bytes includes
marker, length, and
type = 2 for update)

Unfeasible
routes (unlabeled)

Route
advertisement

. . . .

BGP update
message

Additional path attributes

. . . ◄ Additional NLRI

Label | Address prefix ◄ Pad to byte boundary

Multiprotocol
unreachability
path attribute
(with labels)

1 000 0000000000000000000000

Length, in bits (24 + prefix length)
1-byte Subsequent Address Family Identifier (SAFI—4 for MPLS label)
2-byte Address Family Identifier (AFI—1 for IPv4, 2 for IPv6, for example)
3- or 4-byte attribute flags, type, and length (type 15—optional, nontransitive)

FIGURE 6.10

Piggyback labels in BGP

Routes withdrawn using the Unfeasible Routes field (or a multiprotocol path attribute of a type other than MPLS-labeled NLRI) in a BGP Update message are withdrawn for corresponding unlabeled routes. Routes withdrawn using multiprotocol unreachability path attributes of MPLS-labeled NLRI type are withdrawn for corresponding labeled routes.

It is also possible to implicitly withdraw (replace) labels by including a new label in an MPLS multiprotocol reachability path attribute for the same NLRI prefix. The ordering of multiprotocol path attributes is not specified; however, it is a good idea to include explicit route withdrawals in multiprotocol unreachability path attributes earlier than multiprotocol reachability path attributes if both are to be included in the same Update message. This is particularly true when the intent is to explicitly withdraw one label and assert another for the same destination prefix.

Using BGP to piggyback label distribution has the distinct advantage of combining the process of updating a route with updating, or providing, the corresponding label. This effectively eliminates the possibility of inconsistency of routing and labeling within a single LSR. The ability to distribute a label stack as a single operation allows the BGP-speaking LSR to achieve arbitrary scalability in label switching. However, it is not certain that this feature will be immediately advantageous.

The most likely scenario is that an LSR will not use BGP-distributed labels as top-level labels in forwarding packets locally. In the case in which two BGP peers are not directly connected, packets would be forwarded using labels associated with an LSP from the sending peer to the receiving peer. Even in the case in which BGP peers are directly connected, if they are connected via ATM or Frame Relay interfaces, the ATM or Frame Relay "labels" must be established by some other means. Consequently, BGP-distributed labels are likely to be part of a stack having a depth greater than 1 in most cases, even without explicitly including such a stack in BGP Update messages.

There are problems with using BGP to distribute labels when BGP peers are not directly connected. A full discussion of these problems is provided in the section MPLS-BGP in Chapter 5.

Piggyback Label Distribution Using RSVP

The Reservation Protocol (RSVP) might be used to piggyback MPLS labels in two distinct ways: to support explicit routing for unicast LSP setup as defined in RSVP-TE (Awduche et al. w.i.p.) and to support LSP establishment for RSVP sessions as defined in the general RSVP specification (Braden et al. 1997).

Although work to support the more general application started well before the more specific traffic engineering application took the spotlight, specification for support of piggyback of labels for the more general RSVP application—particularly for support of multicast LSP establishment—is not complete. Hence, this book addresses use of RSVP to piggyback labels as defined in RSVP-TE.

RSVP-TE defines creation and maintenance of LSP tunnels using the Shared Explicit (SE) and Fixed Filter (FF) reservation styles. The SE reservation style is generally preferred because it allows for nondisruptive increase in reservation resources and automatic switch-over to a better route.

DEFINED RSVP EXTENSION OBJECTS AND MESSAGES

RSVP-TE defines the following extension objects for use with the base Reservation Protocol:

- Label object
- Label Request object
- Explicit Route object
- Record Route object
- LSP_TUNNEL_IPv4 Session object
- LSP_TUNNEL_IPv6 Session object
- LSP_TUNNEL_IPv4 Sender Template object
- LSP_TUNNEL_IPv6 Sender Template object
- LSP_TUNNEL_IPv4 Filter Specification object
- LSP_TUNNEL_IPv6 Filter Specification object
- Session Attribute object
- TSPEC and FLOWSPEC objects for class of service
- Hello object

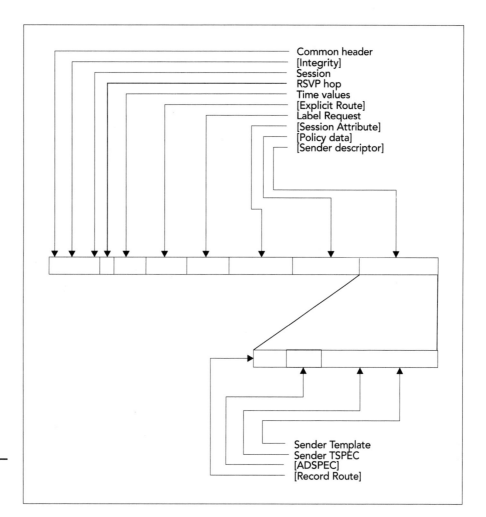

FIGURE 6.11

Path message
format (not to
proportion)

RSVP-TE uses Path, Resv, PathErr, PathTear, and ResvErr messages and
includes the appropriate extension objects. Figure 6.11 shows the format
for a Path message, and Figure 6.12 shows the format for a Resv message
used to establish an LSP tunnel. The procedures using these messages are
described in the following subsections. MPLS-specific error codes and values are listed in Table 6.1.

LSP ESTABLISHMENT

RSVP is used to establish LSP tunnels using downstream on-demand label
distribution. An ingress LSR initiates a request for a specific LSP tunnel

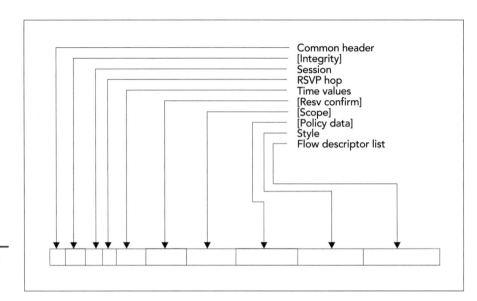

FIGURE 6.12

Resv message format (not to proportion)

TABLE 6.1. RSVP-TE Error Codes and Values for MPLS

Code Explanation	(Code, Value)
Routing problem error code	(24, X)
Bad Explicit Route object	(24, 1)
Bad strict node	(24, 2)
Bad loose node	(24, 3)
Bad initial subobject	(24, 4)
No route available toward destination	(24, 5)
Record Route object syntax error detected	(24, 6)
Loop detected	(24, 7)
MPLS being negotiated, but non-RSVP-capable router stands in the path	(24, 8)
MPLS label allocation failure	(24, 9)
Unsupported layer 3 protocol identifier	(24, 10)
Notify error code	(25, X)
Record Route object too large for MTU	(25, 1)
Record Route notification	(25, 2)

MTU, maximum transmission unit.

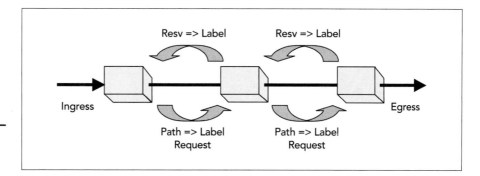

FIGURE 6.13

LSP establish-
ment using
RSVP-TE

using an RSVP Path message and including a session type of LSP_
TUNNEL_IPv4 or LSP_TUNNEL_IPv6 and a Label Request object (Figure
6.13). The Label Request object provides an indication of the network-layer
protocol that is to be carried over this path and may provide a label range
from which a label is requested. The network-layer protocol is needed
because it cannot be assumed that data sent on the LSP is necessarily IP
traffic, and the network layer present after the MPLS shim header is not
provided by the L2 header. Label ranges are needed to support ATM and
Frame Relay.

An ingress LSR may decide to use an explicit route if it knows a route that
has a high likelihood of meeting the tunnel's resource requirements, avoids
network congestion points, takes advantage of underused network
resources, or meets some other policy requirement. The ingress LSR does
this by adding an Explicit Route object (ERO) to the RSVP Path message.
An Explicit Route object specifies the route as a sequence of either strict or
loose abstract nodes. When the ERO is present, each LSR forwards the Path
message along the path the ERO specifies toward the destination.

If a node is incapable of providing a label binding, it sends a PathErr message with an "Unknown object class" error (defined in RFC 2205 [Braden et
al. 1997]). In this way, the ingress LSR will discover if the Label Request
object is not supported end to end via a notification sent by the first node
that does not recognize it.

When the Path message arrives at the egress LSR, that LSR responds to the
message with a Resv message. The egress LSR allocates a label and includes
this label in the Label object it sends in its Resv message response.

Resv messages are sent upstream to the ingress LSR. Intermediate LSRs follow the path state created in processing the Path message, allocating a label and sending it in the Label object in a Resv message to the previous hop. The label each intermediate LSR sends upstream is the label it will use to determine the ILM for this LSP.

Each LSR created a path state using an ERO (if present) or using the previous-hop information determined in Path processing. The egress LSR and all intermediate LSRs use this path state to determine how to forward the Resv message. In this way, Resv processing ensures that label allocation follows the correct path back to the ingress LSR.

When a Resv message, including a Label object, reaches the ingress LSR, the LSP is established. Each node that received Resv messages containing a Label object for this LSP uses that label for forwarding traffic associated with this LSP.

EXPLICITLY ROUTING AN LSP

Explicit routing is accomplished via the Explicit Route object, which each LSR includes in RSVP Path messages. The ERO consists of a concatenation of hops that, taken together, describe the explicitly routed path. Using this object, an LSP follows a predetermined path that is independent of the routed path. The contents of the ERO can be configured or automatically computed using—for example—traffic engineering constraints.

The ERO is generalized through the concepts of an abstract node and loose versus strict hops. An *abstract node* is a set of network elements specified as either an address prefix or an Autonomous System number. If an abstract node consists of a single network element, it is called a *simple* (or *degenerate*) abstract node. Routing of messages within an abstract node is similar to routing for a loose hop, as described next.

Using loosely specified hops allows the ingress LSR to specify an explicit route in the presence of imperfect knowledge about the network. A hop is loosely specified within an ERO by defining the next explicit hop as "loose." This means that the route used to get to the next explicit hop is not important to the entity that defined the ERO. At any LSR, the portion of the ERO that specifies a loose hop may be replaced by a set of one or more explicit hops (which may include both strict and loose hops), based on locally perfected knowledge of the network, for example. Alternatively, the

LSR may elect to forward the message containing the ERO as determined by hop-by-hop routing.

DYNAMICALLY REROUTING AN LSP

A requirement of traffic engineering is the ability to reroute an LSP for a number of reasons, including discovery of a better route, failure of an LSP resource (for example, if a link or node is removed from service or pre-empted), restoration and reoptimization, and so forth. RSVP-TE defines mechanisms to support this capability.

After an LSP has been successfully established, the ingress (or an intermediate) LSR may discover a better route. When this happens, the LSR discovering the better route can dynamically reroute the LSP by simply changing a portion of the Explicit Route object stored in its path state. The ingress LSR can do this for any part of the ERO, up to and including the entire object. An intermediate LSR can only modify that portion of the ERO that was loosely specified in its original path state. Note that this same rerouting behavior also applies when LSPs are modified. For example, if resources required for a specific LSP are increased, the LSP may need to be rerouted using a set of links meeting those increased resource requirements.

If a problem occurs in processing an Explicit Route object (for example, it loops or it is not supported by at least one intermediate router), the ingress LSR is notified via a PathErr message.

It is nearly always desirable to avoid disruption of service in a particular network. For this reason, reroutable LSPs are established using the SE reservation style, which allows make-before-break rerouting with a minimum of double-booking of network resources—especially double-booking of resources along the same path that might cause an erroneous admission control failure.

An LSR uses the combination of the LSP_TUNNEL Session object and the SE reservation style to share LSP resources temporarily between the new and old LSPs at points in common. The LSP_TUNNEL Session object uses the combination of an address of the node that is the egress of the tunnel, a tunnel ID, and an address of the tunnel ingress.

The tunnel ingress appears as two different "senders" because it includes an LSP ID in the new and old Path messages (as part of the Sender Template and Filter Specification objects defined in RSVP. This is necessary in order to obtain labels for a new LSP that is distinct from the old one even at points in common between the old and the new LSPs. In the new LSP establishment, the ingress includes a new LSP ID while it also continues to maintain the old LSP via Path and Resv refresh. The reroute LSP setup otherwise proceeds as it would if it were a new LSP setup. When the Resv message for the new LSP arrives at the ingress LSR, it can switch traffic over to the new LSP and tear down the old one.

DETERMINING THE PATH USED IN ESTABLISHING AN LSP

Adding a Record Route object to the Path message allows the ingress LSR to determine the actual route that an LSP uses. If this object is included in Path messages and supported at all LSRs along the LSP, each LSR will include the address of the outgoing interface on which it forwards a Path message until the Path message reaches the egress LSR. The egress LSR then includes a Record Route object in the Resv message, and the object is added to in the same way on the reverse path.

The Record Route object and the Explicit Route object may be used together to loosely specify the path to be used in (for example) a traffic engineering LSP and then to effectively pin this route with a strict explicit route. This is accomplished by including the Record Route object in the Path message in which the loose Explicit Route object is provided. When the corresponding Resv message is received by the ingress LSR, it can determine the exact path used and construct the corresponding strict Explicit Route object. This can be very useful if the ingress does not have perfect knowledge of the network topology and yet needs to establish an LSP that will not be potentially disrupted by switching over to a better path.

An ingress LSR can also use the Record Route object to request notification from the network concerning changes to the routing path and to detect loops.

IDENTIFYING AND DIAGNOSING AN LSP

Identifying an LSP (for example, for diagnostic purposes) is accomplished by including the Session Attribute object in a Path message. This object also contains preemption and hold priorities and flags to control the LSP.

PREEMPTING AN EXISTING LSP

An LSP setup request with a setup priority that is higher (lower numerical value) than an existing LSP's hold priority can preempt the LSP with a lower hold priority in the event that sufficient resources to satisfy the new setup request are not otherwise available.

Label Distribution Protocol

Since LDP is a stand-alone protocol for distributing labels, it does not rely on the ubiquitous presence of any specific routing protocols at every hop along an LSP path in order to establish an LSP. Thus, LDP is useful in situations in which an LSP is to be set up across LSRs that may not all support a common piggybacked approach to distributing labels. For the purposes of a discussion of stand-alone label distribution, CR-LDP is treated as an extension to LDP that incorporates explicit routing and resource allocation.

LDP uses TCP as a transport protocol, allowing for reliable in-order delivery of its control messages. This allows LDP to make assumptions about LSP state based on the status of the TCP transport. The state of all LSPs is assumed to be valid for as long as the TCP connection is valid.

LDP has four categories of defined messages and an additional category for vendor private and experimental messages (Table 6.2). In addition, LDP and CR-LDP define status codes, shown in Table 6.3, and typ-length-value encoded objects (TLVs), shown in Table 6.4. In these two tables, values defined by CR-LDP are shaded.

LDP SESSION ESTABLISHMENT

Prior to establishing any LSPs, it is first necessary for each LSR along the intended path to establish an LDP session with adjacent LSRs that are also along the intended path.

LDP peers discover adjacent LDP peers via Hello messages sent out on all LDP-enabled interfaces. Hello messages are IP multicast to the "all routers this subnet" IP multicast address (0xe0000002 or 224.0.0.2) using UDP, and the implementation must be able to direct sending on specific interfaces and determine which interface a Hello message was received on. When a

TABLE 6.2. LDP General Message Types

Type	Description and Values (decimal; hexadecimal)
Discovery	Used to announce the presence of an LSR adjacency at a network interface
Hello	256; 0x0100
Session control	Used to establish, maintain, and terminate sessions between two LDP peers
Initialization	512; 0x0200
KeepAlive	513; 0x0201
Advertisement	Used to create, change, and delete label mappings for FECs and address bindings for LSRs
Address	768; 0x0300
Address Withdraw	769; 0x0301
Label Mapping	1024; 0x0400
Label Request	1025; 0x0401
Label Withdraw	1026; 0x0402
Notification	Used to provide advisory or error information
Notification	1; 0x0001
Extension messages	
Vendor Private	15,872 through 16,127; 0x3e00 through 0x3eff
Experimental	16,128 through 16,383; 0x3f00 through 0x3fff

Hello message is received on an LDP-enabled interface, the LSR establishes an adjacency and each adjacent LSR initiates either a passive or active role in establishing a TCP connection and LDP session.

For ATM and Frame Relay interfaces, LDP exchanges label range information during the session initialization process. Label ranges established during session initialization are assumed to be valid for the duration of the session.

Once an LDP session is established for all peers along the path of an LSP, LSP establishment can proceed.

LSP ESTABLISHMENT

LDP may be used to establish LSPs using downstream unsolicited or downstream on-demand label distribution (Figure 6.14).

In downstream unsolicited label distribution, each LSR along the path may send a Label Mapping message to its upstream peer relative to any specific FEC. In independent control mode, these messages may all happen at

TABLE 6.3. LDP and CR-LDP Status Codes

Status Code	Fatal?	Forward?	Status Value (decimal; hexadecimal)
Success	No	No	0; 0×00000000
Bad LDP Identifier	Yes	No	1; 0×00000001
Bad Protocol Version	Yes	No	2; 0×00000002
Bad PDU Length	Yes	No	3; 0×00000003
Unknown Message Type	No	?	4; 0×00000004
Bad Message Length	Yes	No	5; 0×00000005
Unknown TLV	No	?	6; 0×00000006
Bad TLV Length	Yes	No	7; 0×00000007
Malformed TLV Value	Yes	No	8; 0×00000008
Hold Timer Expired	Yes	No	9; 0×00000009
Shutdown	Yes	No	10; 0×0000000a
Loop Detected	No	Yes	11; 0×0000000b
Unknown FEC	No	Yes	12; 0×0000000c
No Route	No	Yes	13; 0×0000000d
No Label Resources	No	No	14; 0×0000000e
Label Resources Available	No	No	15; 0×0000000f
Session Rejected, No Hello	Yes	No	16; 0×00000010
Session Rejected, Parameters Advertisement Mode	Yes	No	17; 0×00000011
Session Rejected, Parameters Max PDU Length	Yes	No	18; 0×00000012
Session Rejected, Parameters Label Range	Yes	No	19;0×00000013
KeepAlive Timer Expired	Yes	No	20; 0×00000014
Label Request Aborted	No	No	21; 0×00000015
Missing Message Parameters	No	Yes	22; 0×00000016
Unsupported Address Family	No	Yes	23; 0×00000017
Session Rejected, Bad KeepAlive Time	Yes	No	24; 0×00000018
Internal Error	Yes	No	25; 0×00000019
Bad Explicit Routing Error	No	Yes	67,108,865; 0×04000001
Bad Strict Node Error	No	Yes	67,108,866; 0×04000002
Bad Loose Node Error	No	Yes	67,108,867; 0×04000003
Bad Initial ER-Hop Error	No	Yes	67,108,868; 0×04000004
Resource Unavailable	No	Yes	67,108,869; 0×04000005
Traffic Parameters Unavailable	No	Yes	67,108,870; 0×04000006
LSP Preempted	No	Yes	67,108,871; 0×04000007
Modify Request Not Supported	No	Yes	67,108,872; 0×04000008
Setup Abort	No	No	67,108,886; 0×04000015

PDU, protocol data unit; TLV, type-length-value; ER, explicit route.

TABLE 6.4. LDP and CR-LDP TLV Objects

TLV Object and Element Type	Value (decimal; hexadecimal)
FEC	256; 0x0100
Wild card	1; 0x01
Prefix	2; 0x02
Host Address	3; 0x03
CR-LSP	4; 0x04
Address List	257; 0x0101
Hop Count	259; 0x0103
Path Vector	260; 0x0104
Generic Label	512; 0x0200
ATM Label	513; 0x0201
Frame Relay Label	514; 0x0202
Status	768; 0x0300
Extended Status	769; 0x0301
Returned PDU	770; 0x0302
Returned Message	771; 0x0303
Common Hello Parameters	1024; 0x0400
Transport Address	1025; 0x0401
Configuration Sequence Number	1026; 0x0402
IPv6 Transport Address	1027; 0x0403
Common Session Parameters	1280; 0x0500
ATM Session Parameters	1281; 0x0501
Frame Relay Session Parameters	1282; 0x0502
Label Request Message ID	1536; 0x0600
Explicit Route	2048; 0x0800
IPv4 Prefix ER-Hop	2049; 0x0801
IPv6 Prefix ER-Hop	2050; 0x0802
Autonomous System Number ER-Hop	2051; 0x0803
LSP-ID ER-Hop	2052; 0x0804
Traffic Parameters	2064; 0x0810
Preemption	2080; 0x0820
LSPID	2081; 0x0821
Resource Class	2082; 0x0822
Route Pinning	2083; 0x0823
Vendor Private	15,872 through 16,127; 0x3e00 through 0x3eff
Experimental	16,128 through 16,383; 0x3f00 through 0x3fff

LDP reserves UDP and TCP ports 646 as well-known ports for use exclusively by LDP.

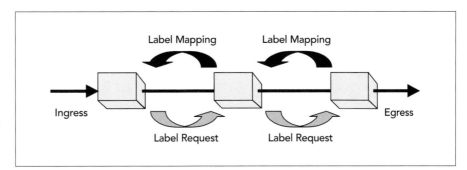

FIGURE 6.14

LSP establish-
ment using LDP
or CR-LDP

roughly the same time, whereas in ordered control mode, the process of propagating Label Mapping messages starts at the egress LSR. In downstream unsolicited label distribution, Label Request messages are the exception rather than the rule.

In downstream on-demand distribution, an LSR initiates a request for a specific LSP using a Label Request message. The Label Request message provides an indication of the FEC for which a label mapping is requested. In ordered control mode, this LSR would be the ingress for the LSP. In independent control mode, it could be any LSR along the LSP associated with the FEC.

Basic LDP is primarily intended to establish best-effort LSPs based on the routing topology. In this sense, LDP may be used in a manner similar to the way in which BGP is used to piggyback labels—doing so independent of any specific routing protocol, however. CR-LDP provides extensions to LDP that are useful in establishing better-than-best-effort LSPs or LSPs that follow paths not determined by the routing topology.

An ingress LSR may decide to use an explicit route if it knows a route that has a high likelihood of meeting the tunnel's resource requirements, avoids network congestion points, takes advantage of underused network resources, or meets some other policy requirement.

The ingress LSR does this by adding an Explicit Route TLV (ER-TLV) to the LDP Label Request message. Use of an ER-TLV to establish an LSP requires use of downstream on-demand distribution and ordered control mode. An Explicit Route TLV specifies the route as a sequence of either strict or loose abstract nodes.

When the ER-TLV is present, each LSR forwards the Label Request message along the path the ER-TLV specifies toward the destination. If a node is incapable of providing a label binding, it sends a Notification message with an appropriate status code (defined either in Andersson et al. 2000 or Jamoussi 2000). In this way, the ingress LSR will discover if the label request is not supported end to end via a notification sent by the first node that is not able to support it.

When a Label Request message arrives at the egress LSR, that LSR responds to the message with a Label Mapping message. The egress LSR allocates a label and includes this label in the Label Mapping message it sends in response.

Label Mapping messages are sent upstream toward the ingress LSR. In downstream on-demand distribution with ordered control mode, intermediate LSRs follow the LSP state created in processing the Label Request message, allocating a label and sending it in the Label Mapping message to the upstream LSR. The label that each intermediate LSR sends upstream is the label it will use to determine the ILM for this LSP for all interfaces through which the upstream LDP peer is adjacent.

Each LSR creates LSP state using an ER-TLV (if present) or using the information about the requesting LDP peer from Label Request message processing. The egress LSR and all intermediate LSRs use this LSP state to determine how to forward the Label Mapping message. In this way, Label Request processing ensures that label allocation and Label Mapping message propagation follow the correct path back to the ingress LSR.

When a Label Mapping message for a requested label reaches the ingress LSR, the LSP is established. Each node that received Label Mapping messages containing a label for this LSP uses that label for forwarding traffic associated with this LSP.

Once LSPs exist, the following rules, in the order given, are used to map a given packet to an LSP.

1. If there is exactly one LSP that has a Host Address FEC element that is identical to the packet's destination address, the packet is mapped to that LSP.

2. If there are multiple LSPs, each containing a Host Address FEC element that is identical to the packet's destination address, the packet is

mapped to one of those LSPs. The procedure for selecting one of those LSPs is beyond the scope of this chapter.

3. If a packet matches exactly one LSP, the packet is mapped to that LSP.

4. If a packet matches multiple LSPs, it is mapped to the LSP whose matching prefix is the longest. If there is no one LSP whose matching prefix is longest, the packet is mapped to one from the set of LSPs whose matching prefix is longer than the others. The procedure for selecting one of those LSPs is beyond the scope of this chapter.

5. If it is known that a packet must traverse a particular egress router, and there is an LSP that has a Prefix FEC element that is an address of that router, then the packet is mapped to that LSP. This information might be known, for example, as a consequence of running a link-state routing protocol (such as IS-IS or OSPF) or from the next-hop attribute of a BGP route advertisement.

EXPLICITLY ROUTING AN LSP

Explicit routing is accomplished via the Explicit Route TLV, which each LSR includes in Label Request messages. The ER-TLV consists of a concatenation of hops that, taken together, describe the explicitly routed path. Using this TLV, an LSP follows a predetermined path that is independent of the routed path. The contents of the ER-TLV can be configured or automatically computed using (for example) traffic engineering constraints.

The ER-TLV is generalized through the use of the concepts of an abstract node, and loose versus strict hops. An *abstract node* is a set of network elements specified as either an address prefix or an Autonomous System number. If an abstract node consists of a single network element, it is called a *simple* (or *degenerate*) abstract node. Routing of messages within an abstract node is similar to routing for a loose hop, as described next.

Using loosely specified hops allows the ingress LSR to specify an explicit route in the presence of imperfect knowledge about the network. A hop is loosely specified within an ER-TLV by defining the next explicit hop as "loose." This means that the route used to get to the next explicit hop is not important to the entity that defined the ER-TLV. At any LSR, the portion of the ER-TLV that specifies a loose hop may be replaced by a set of one or more explicit hops (which may include both strict and loose hops), based on locally perfected knowledge of the network, for example. Alternatively, the LSR may elect to forward the message containing the ER-TLV as determined by hop-by-hop routing.

DYNAMICALLY REROUTING AN LSP

A requirement of traffic engineering is the ability to reroute an LSP for a number of reasons, including discovery of a better route, failure of an LSP resource (for example, if a link or node is removed from service or preempted), restoration and reoptimization, and so forth. CR-LDP defines mechanisms to support this capability. Rerouting is, in general, automatic for best-effort, hop-by-hop LSPs using LDP.

After an LSP has been successfully established, the ingress (or an intermediate) LSR may discover a better route. When this happens, the LSR discovering the better route can dynamically reroute the LSP by simply changing a portion of the Explicit Route TLV stored in its path state and initiating a Label Request message. As the originator of an LSP, the ingress LSR can do this for any part of the ER-LDP, up to and including the entire TLV. An intermediate LSR can modify the portion of the LSP that is immediately downstream from it in some cases. For example, if it was specified as loose in the original ER-TLV, the LSR can forward LSP messages to a different peer. The same is true if the LSR is specified in the ER-TLV as an abstract node and the current best route changes to include a different peer within the same abstract node. Note that this same rerouting behavior also applies when LSPs are modified. For example, if resources required for a specific LSP are increased, the LSP may need to be rerouted using a set of links meeting those increased resource requirements.

If a problem occurs in processing an Explicit Route TLV (for example, it loops or it is not supported by at least one intermediate router), the ingress LSR is notified via a Notification message.

When using CR-LDP, it is possible to reroute a portion of an LSP due to discovery of a better route by using the same LSP identifier (LSP-ID) as the last explicit route hop in a reroute Label Request message. The LSP-ID is a combination of an interface address of the ingress LSR and a locally unique identifier generated at that LSR. When a downstream peer recognizes the LSP-ID of an already existing LSP and determines that this is the last explicitly routed hop, it simply merges the new LSP with the old and returns a label mapping. On receiving a label mapping for the new LSP segment, the Label Request initiator can release the label for the old LSP to the downstream peer for that LSP. This Label Release message is propagated to the LSP merge point downstream (or to the original egress), releasing resources associated with the old LSP at each LSR prior to the merge point. The merge-point LSR releases the label for the old LSP, but will determine that it still has an upstream source for this LSP and will not release other LSP resources or downstream labels.

EXPLICIT STACKING OF AN LSP

The LSP-ID explicit hop type can also be used to stack LSPs. If an ingress LSR originates a Label Request message including an ER-TLV with an LSP-ID that is not the last explicit hop, the LSR processing that explicit hop forwards the label mapping to the next explicit hop using the specified LSP. When that LSR receives a Label Mapping message, the label associated with that message will be pushed onto the label stack prior to pushing on the label for the specified LSP. Note that for this to work, the LSR processing the explicit hop with an LSP-ID must be an ingress for that LSP.

IDENTIFYING AND DIAGNOSING AN LSP

An LSP is identified by its LSP-ID in CR-LDP. Hop-by-hop routed best-effort LSPs as established using the base LDP protocol are identified by label and FEC at each LSR and have no global identification.

PREEMPTING AN EXISTING LSP

CR-LDP defines the optional use of setup and hold priorities. If the setup priority is defined for a CR-LDP Label Request message and the setup priority is higher (lower numerical value) than an existing LSP's hold priority, the new Label Request can preempt the LSP with a lowest hold priority in the event that sufficient resources to satisfy the new setup request are not otherwise available.

6.5 Loops and Loop Mitigation, Detection, and Prevention

Loops are most often formed as a result of inconsistent information in a distributed route computation. This is roughly analogous to an exercise in passing the buck. If router R1 believes that the shortest path is via R2 and R3, and R2 believes the shortest path is via R3, and R3 believes the shortest path is via R1 and R2, then data will loop until all of the routers are again synchronized in their shortest-path computations.

Impact of Looping

A loop may affect either data traffic or control traffic. Depending on how control messages are forwarded, the same problems that would cause looping of data traffic will also cause looping of control traffic. Protocol designers and network engineers use careful consideration in designing control protocols to ensure that the presence of a loop in the control plane will not prevent loop detection and removal.

DATA TRAFFIC

The key issues regarding looping data traffic in MPLS are as follows:

- The relatively low latency at each hop (which acts to increase the rate at which looping traffic produces a ramp-up in resources consumed)
- The possibility that a loop might occur using a medium with no loop mitigation approach in place

Loop mitigation is discussed later. In general, it is highly desirable that the network not allow persistent looping of data traffic.

CONTROL MESSAGES

Looping of control messages occurs in much the same way as looping data messages but can be both better and worse than looping in the data path. Looping of control messages in MPLS signaling generally occurs under the same conditions that would cause looping of corresponding data traffic. Thus, the fact that the control messages are not able to complete setup of a looping LSP helps to prevent formation of data loops (although data may be being "black-holed" instead—that is, delivered to some point where further delivery is not feasible and data is simply dropped). But control messages are processed using the slow path and consume a somewhat scarcer resource. Thus, allowing control messages to loop could result in an implementation's being unable to recover from a network change because of backlogged control messages and functions.

In addition, in the presence of hierarchical LSPs, the failure of lower-level LSPs to successfully forward control messages associated with higher-level LSPs can result in significant network outages and potential pathological behavior. To a high-level LSP, lower-level LSPs form the links over which both data and control messages are forwarded. These links—being based on MPLS control themselves—take time to become reestablished after a change. For this reason, it is a good idea to allow for delay in reestablishing LSPs after a change when these LSPs depend on establishment of lower-level LSPs.

Loop Mitigation

Loop mitigation is the process of reducing the impact of looping data on other data in the network. IP Time to Live (TTL) and fair queuing are examples of loop mitigation techniques. Loop mitigation is useful in helping the network to survive short-duration loops in data traffic paths. For this reason, loop detection can be considered a loop mitigation technique.

IP TTL relies on the routing requirement that each router decrement the TTL by at least 1 and not forward a packet with a TTL that is less than or equal to zero. Use of TTL results in discard of looping packets after they have been in the network an "unreasonable" amount of time. Typically, TTL defaults to some power of 2. TTL is not available as a loop mitigation technique in technologies that rely on some other approach to prevent formation of loops. An example is ATM switches, which relied originally on end-to-end signaling (the equivalent of MPLS ordered control) to prevent forming a virtual circuit with a loop in it. When ATM switches are used as LSRs, therefore, TTL is not sufficient for loop mitigation.

Use of multiple queues in a fair-queuing arrangement is a way to isolate traffic in different queues from the effects of looping traffic. Looping packets will naturally be enqueued in the same queue that they were placed in previously, thus limiting the impact to those queues. Where specific interesting queuing techniques are in use, however, this effect can spread. For example, if looping traffic in a high-priority queue results in the higher-priority traffic being demoted into lower-priority queues, the impact of looping will affect lower-priority traffic as well. ATM switches often have significant advantages in terms of queuing as a form of loop mitigation, particularly in implementations that support per-VC queuing.

The absence of a loop mitigation approach allows looping data to multiply itself arbitrarily and can effectively shut down the network during even a short-term looping condition.

Looping of control messages can be mitigated using hop count. Hop count acts as a reverse TTL: Hop count is incremented at each hop and, when it exceeds some configured amount, the control message is dropped. MPLS control message looping can also be mitigated via merging. A looping Label Request message will not typically be forwarded beyond the first merge point at which it is received (at least the second time). This is because the merge point will already have an outstanding label request and can merge any labels it allocates to upstream peers using the label it expects to receive corresponding to the downstream portion of the merged LSP.

Loop Detection

In general, looping of control messages is detectable using a number of approaches, as long as the specific approach chosen is consistently supported at each LSR along the path chosen to establish an LSP.

Looping control messages can be detected using a simple hop count that is incremented as the message is forwarded. When this hop count exceeds some configured value, the control message is dropped and further looping is prevented. However, this does not result in actual loop detection unless a message is returned to the sender, allowing the originator to detect the presence of a loop. An example of such a message might be a Label Release message (in LDP) with a Loop Detected status code.

Looping control messages can also be detected using a path vector TLV (in LDP) or Record Route object (in RSVP-TE). Once such an object is received containing the ID of the local LSR, the looping of the control message is detected and further looping of this specific control message is prevented. The existence of a loop is detected by the LSR at which the loop starts (this will be the first LSR to see that it is already in the path vector or RRO).

Loop Prevention

Looping of data messages can be prevented by simply not using an LSP until it is determined to be loop free. This is the actual behavior when ordered control mode is used or when ingress LSRs do not forward data packets along an LSP until a Label Mapping message is received with a known hop count.

Looping of control messages is prevented when LSP signaling incorporates the use of LSP merging. This is the default condition using LDP, for example, to establish a best-effort hop-by-hop LSP in networks including merge-capable LSRs. Looping of control messages is prevented because (irrespective of the control mode) it is not necessary to propagate a control message beyond the merge point in order to establish a best-effort LSP.

Looping of control messages using independent control mode is prevented because generation of one control message is not consequent on (is independent of) receipt of another until a known hop count is provided by an egress LSR. Each message (associated with setup of a single LSP) is propagated exactly once, even when a loop exists, irrespective of whether merging is supported. Once a known hop count is provided, a looping control message is not forwarded further if the hop count exceeds some configured maximum value. Similarly, looping of control messages in ordered control mode is prevented once such a loop is detected using either a path vector or a Record Route object mechanism.

Looping of control messages can also be prevented through the use of a *colored thread* approach, which is very similar to the approach that prevents looping control messages in the merging best-effort case. Each control message is propagated with a *color* (a value assigned by, and unique to, the thread initiator), and a control message is not propagated further if an identical control message (with the same color) has already been forwarded at an LSR. This approach is defined in Ohba et al. (w.i.p.).

References

Andersson, Loa, Paul Doolan, Nancy Feldman, Andre Fredette, and Bob Thomas. 2001 (January). LDP specification. RFC 3036. Available at http://www.isi.edu/in-notes/rfc3036.txt.

Awduche, Daniel O., Lou Berger, Der-Hwa Gan, Tony Li, Vijay Srinivasan, and George Swallow. RSVP-TE: Extensions to RSVP for LSP tunnels; a work in progress.

Awduche, Daniel O., Joe Malcolm, Johnson Agogbua, Mike O'Dell, and Jim McManus. 1999 (September). Requirements for traffic engineering over MPLS. RFC 2702. Available at http://www.isi.edu/in-notes/rfc2702.txt.

Bates, Tony, Ravi Chandra, Dave Katz, and Yakov Rekhter. 1998 (February). Multiprotocol extensions for BGP-4. RFC 2283. Available at http://www.isi.edu/in-notes/rfc2283.txt.

Black, Uyless. *Data Link Protocols*. Englewood Cliffs, NJ: Prentice Hall, 1993.

Braden, Bob, Lixia Zhang, Steve Berson, Shai Herzog, and Sugih Jamin. 1997 (September). Resource ReSerVation Protocol (RSVP)—version 1 functional specification. RFC 2205. Available at http://www.isi.edu/in-notes/rfc2205.txt.

Comer, Douglas E. *Computer Networks and Internets*. Upper Saddle River, NJ: Prentice Hall, 1997.

Grossman, Dan, and Juha Heinanen. 1999 (September). Multiprotocol encapsulation over ATM Adaptation Layer 5. RFC 2684. Available at http://www.isi.edu/in-notes/rfc2684.txt.

IANA (Internet Assigned Numbers Authority). Undated a. Ether types. Available at http://www.isi.edu/in-notes/iana/assignments/ethernet-numbers.

IANA (Internet Assigned Numbers Authority). Undated b. Protocol numbers. Available at http://www.isi.edu/in-notes/iana/assignments/protocol-numbers.

Jamoussi, Bilel, ed. Constraint-based LSP setup using LDP; a work in progress.

Ohba, Yoshihiro, Yasuhiro Katsube, Eric Rosen, and Paul Doolan. MPLS loop prevention mechanism; a work in progress.

Perkins, Charles. 1996a (October). IP encapsulation within IP. RFC 2003. Available at http://www.isi.edu/in-notes/rfc2003.txt.

Perkins, Charles. 1996b (October). Minimal encapsulation within IP. RFC 2004. Available at http://www.isi.edu/in-notes/rfc2004.txt.

Postel, Jon, ed. 1981 (September). Internet Protocol. RFC 791. Available at http://www.isi.edu/in-notes/rfc791.txt.

Rekhter, Yakov, and Tony Li. 1995 (March). A Border Gateway Protocol 4 (BGP-4). RFC 1771. Available at http://www.isi.edu/in-notes/rfc1771.txt.

Rekhter, Yakov, and Eric C. Rosen. Carrying label information in BGP-4; a work in progress.

Reynolds, Joyce K., and Jon Postel. 1994 (October). Assigned numbers. RFC 1700. Available at http://www.isi.edu/in-notes/rfc1700.txt.

Simpson, William, ed. 1994 (July). The Point-to-Point Protocol (PPP). STD

51/RFC 1661. Available at http://www.isi.edu/in-notes/rfc1661.txt.

Simpson, William, ed. 1996 (August). PPP link quality monitoring. RFC 1989. Available at http://www.isi.edu/in-notes/rfc1989.txt.

Simpson, William, ed. 1997 (May). PPP vendor extensions. RFC 2153. Available at http://www.isi.edu/in-notes/rfc2153.txt.

7

SERVICES

Man's mind, stretched to a new idea, never
goes back to its original dimensions.
•*Oliver Wendell Holmes*

This chapter describes how services are provided using MPLS. Included in this description is a high-level overview of the pieces used to provide these services, including specific protocol support functions. Specifics of the protocols and components of MPLS used in providing these services are discussed in greater detail in earlier sections of this book.

7.1 Basic Services

 Basic services in MPLS are effectively enabled using hop-by-hop LSPs established using LDP in the intranet (IGP) case and MPLS-BGP in the Internet (EGP) case.

Using LDP

In the IGP/LDP case, and assuming that the goal is to establish a best-effort LSP for each route table entry at each LSR, the process is as follows:

    1. Route advertisements build up the local LSR's picture of the network.

2. While the routing function builds a table of routes, the LDP function establishes sessions with peers as it discovers their adjacency.

3. As the routing function within the LSR converges on a routing topology, the LDP function begins distributing labels for each route to each peer with which it has established a session and for which the peer is not the next hop.[1]

Note that this process assumes that label distribution is downstream unsolicited. In the event that the label distribution mode is actually downstream on-demand, labels are distributed as described except that the local LSR requests labels from the next-hop LSR peer for each route table entry.

If conservative label retention is used, the LSR retains those labels that it will use and releases those that it will not use. Otherwise, any number of labels may be retained, up to and including all labels received. Using the labels retained specifically for each given FEC's next hop, an LSR constructs an NHLFE and an FEC-to-NHLFE map (FTN) if the LSR is an ingress for the LSP, an Incoming Label Map (ILM) if the LSR is not an ingress for the LSP and will receive only labeled packets for the corresponding FEC, or both if the LSR expects to receive both labeled and unlabeled packets from upstream routers that will be merged onto the same LSP.

If the LSR has constructed an FTN, it may act as the ingress for any unlabeled packets it receives by using a matching NHLFE (if a valid one exists).[2] An LSR may act as an egress for labeled packets it receives having an ILM and no matching NHLFE. An LSR is expected to perform some label operation (push, pop, or swap) if it receives a labeled packet for which it has both an ILM and a matching NHLFE. An LSR may be expected to forward unlabeled packets as unlabeled packets if it has no FTN or no matching NHLFE.

As route table entries are added, removed, or changed, the LSR takes corresponding label distribution actions (advertising, requesting a new label or

---

1. It is possible to distribute labels in this case as well. However, there is little point because anything received with that label should be dropped rather than returned.

2. An NHLFE is only "matching" if it is a valid and active NHLFE.

withdrawing the request, releasing the existing invalid label). If an LSR loses a peer (because the peer session is terminated, perhaps because the adjacency is lost), it invalidates all corresponding labels.

Using BGP

With BGP, labels are distributed piggyback on BGP route advertisements (using BGP Update messages). The label stack distributed as a part of a BGP route remains valid until that route is explicitly replaced or invalidated based on BGP routing. In practice, the behavior is much like the behavior for LDP because the two protocols have a great deal in common.

7.2 Quality of Service: Premium Services

Using the Integrated Services Model

Both RSVP-TE and CR-LDP support the Integrated Services QoS model and can support this model when used in tandem. RSVP-TE is a more natural fit than CR-LDP for this usage because RSVP was designed with Integrated Services model support in mind. However, the same objects—with relatively minor alterations, at most—are used in CR-LDP, thus providing a seamless adaptation between the two approaches.

The Path message (in RSVP-TE) or the Label Request message (in CR-LDP) carries the resource requirements for an LSP intended to support the Integrated Services QoS model. In each case, when this information arrives at an egress, a corresponding response is generated (Resv for RSVP-TE, and Label Mapping for CR-LDP) and LSR resources are committed during the process of propagating the response back to the originator. Clearly, in both cases, the downstream on-demand label distribution and ordered control modes are used. Also, in either case, implementations are free to commit resources during the request phase (the portion of the signaling process during which label requests are being propagated downstream).

Using the Differentiated Services Model

Support for the Differentiated Services QoS model can be achieved via establishment of specific L-LSPs,[3] each of which is administratively associated with some defined per-hop behavior (PHB). It can also be achieved via establishment of a single E-LSP (see footnote 3) for each Ordered Aggregate of PHBs, allowing the use of configured values of the Experimental (EXP) bits to determine which specific PHB is to be used for any labeled packet.

An E-LSP is distinguished from an L-LSP by the former's use of the EXP bits in the generic label format. The Cell Loss Priority (CLP) field in ATM and the Discard Eligibility (DE) field in Frame Relay are used similarly, though with less effect, for E-LSPs in their respective technologies. With L-LSPs, the label itself implies the behavior that applies to packets within the given LSP.

Either RSVP-TE or LDP may be used to establish LSP support for the Differentiated Services model. In the RSVP-TE case, new Class of Service (COS) objects are provided to allow for setup of an LSP for this purpose, effectively establishing an LSP for classes of best-effort service.

7.3 Traffic Engineering

Traffic engineering (TE) is the process of optimizing the performance of operational networks. In doing this, TE skirts the ragged edge of computational intractability in an effort to extend the utilization of network resources. TE uses both computation and heuristics to achieve a good-enough utilization factor for a given set of network resources and traffic conditions. Because heuristics produce an inexact solution to the TE problem, the

---

3. L-LSP and E-LSP stand for Label-only-inferred-PSC LSP and EXP-inferred-PSC LSP, respectively. EXP refers to the Experimental bits field in the generic label, the Cell Loss Priority (CLP) field in the ATM header, or the Discard Eligibility (DE) field in the Frame Relay header. PSC stands for PHB Scheduling Class, and PHB stands for per-hop behavior. See Le Faucheur et al. (w.i.p.) for details on how Differentiated Services is supported in MPLS. I suspect that many proponents of Differentiated Services may have migrated into the field out of frustration at the lack of acronyms being used in other standards organizations and bodies.

survival of service providers in the competition to offer low-cost, high-quality services will depend in a large measure on the long-term effectiveness of the heuristics chosen by each service provider.

The key goals in TE are to maximize network efficiency and total data "good put." Priorities within the "good put" category are as follows (approximately in order):

- Minimization of packet loss
- Minimization of delay, maximization of throughput, and enforcement of Service Level Agreements (SLAs)
- Bounded delay variation, loss ratio, and maximum transfer delay

Specific goals for network efficiency revolve around ensuring that the average utilization of network resources is as close to 100% as possible while minimum and maximum utilization of individual resources are as close to the average as possible.

Both goals are affected by congestion; thus, avoidance of congestion is of paramount importance. Problems associated with congestion are made worse by inefficient use of network resources. These problems are directly addressable using TE.

The TE model consists of a connected network, performance monitoring feedback, and a management and control system. The traffic engineer determines the current state of the network (via performance monitoring), analyzes the traffic characteristics and trends, and attempts to control the network in such a way as to alter the current state to one that maximizes the desired characteristics of the network and accommodates existing traffic characteristics and trends. This process is a continuously ongoing effort.

To minimize the amount of operator involvement in the TE model, it is desirable to minimize the operator's involvement in modifying traffic management and routing parameters and in modifying the way in which the system's use of resources is artificially constrained. A desirable solution is one that is both scalable and resilient.

Interior gateway routing protocol capabilities are not up to the task. In fact, prevalent IGPs contribute to congestion because they are effectively designed to develop a consistent view of the topology that results in traffic being forwarded dominantly along shortest paths. As a result, shortest-path routes are likely to be highly congested while similar routes are likely to be underutilized.

An important factor in the long-term effectiveness of a TE solution is system responsiveness to changes in traffic conditions and corresponding measurement of resource utilization.

The Role of MPLS

MPLS is useful for TE in the specific aspects of measurement and dynamic control of Internet traffic. Because of the high cost of networking resources and the competitive environment that each service provider faces, dynamic performance optimization in service provider networks is a critical factor in determining a service provider's ability to survive in the industry.

One important aspect of TE is the introduction of simple load-balancing techniques. However, traffic engineering also needs to take into account other factors affecting total income production from use of the service provider's network. This requires mechanisms for supporting more complicated policies than a simple load-balancing scheme. MPLS provides a means for effecting more complex TE solutions at a potentially lower cost than alternative technologies.

MPLS offers dynamic mechanisms for establishing explicitly routed LSPs that can operate independently of IGP-determined routes. This reduces the impact that limitations in routing protocol behavior have on congestion in the network. Because MPLS mechanisms are dynamic, LSPs can be established with desirable resiliency and can be reoptimized as needed.

Specific attractive features of MPLS are as follows:

- Explicit label-switched paths that are not constrained by the destination-based forwarding paradigm can be easily created through manual administrative action or through automated action by the underlying protocols.
- LSPs can be efficiently maintained.
- Traffic trunks can be mapped onto LSPs, and traffic trunk attributes can be used to modify the behavior of the trunks.
- Resource attributes can be used to constrain the placement of LSPs (and associated traffic trunks).

- Traffic can be both aggregated and deaggregated.

- MPLS may offer significantly lower overhead relative to competing TE alternatives.

How Traffic Engineering Works

A TE solution needs to provide a means for directing traffic along paths that would not be taken using the routing infrastructure alone.

ATM and Frame Relay virtual circuits (VCs) have been successfully used as TE solutions to date. Use of virtual circuits in an overlay topology allows VC-based routing, explicit administrative configuration of VC paths, path compression, admission control, traffic shaping and policing, and VC survivability.

Using virtual circuits thus allows many TE functions to be accomplished with today's networks.

Equipping MPLS with a similar virtual circuit capability is important for future network TE needs. MPLS offers the ability to provide an integrated overlay model at a lower cost than existing ATM and Frame Relay equipment. MPLS also offers the opportunity to automate some of the traffic engineering functions.

The difficulty in realizing a TE solution using MPLS is the hierarchical nature of the mapping of traffic onto LSPs in a TE model. Ultimately, the traffic engineer wants to create traffic trunks to shunt traffic in the network in such a way as to produce efficient utilization. These traffic trunks would be realized using explicitly routed LSPs in order to achieve independence from the underlying routing infrastructure. However, traffic is mapped onto LSPs using forwarding equivalence classes (FECs). Thus, it is necessary to determine the FEC-to-traffic-trunk mapping that will produce the most efficient mapping of traffic to traffic trunks and then onto the overlay of explicitly routed LSPs.

To do this, TE over MPLS requires

- Traffic trunk definitions in terms of the set of forwarding equivalence classes that will be associated with each traffic trunk

- Traffic trunk behavioral attributes

TABLE 7.1. Traffic Trunk Operations

Action	Description
Establish	Create a traffic trunk instance
Activate	Begin passing traffic via this traffic trunk instance
Deactivate	Cease passing traffic via this traffic trunk instance
Modify	Change attributes of this traffic trunk instance
Reroute	Redetermine the path used by this traffic trunk instance
Destroy	Remove a traffic trunk instance and free associated resources

- Network resource attributes
- A plan for selecting the explicit route to be used for a set of traffic trunks to achieve a "good enough" maximization function given the constraints of the traffic trunk behavioral attributes and network resource attributes
- Signaling to establish explicitly routed LSPs for the set of traffic trunks

LSP-based traffic trunks are inherently unidirectional; however, bidirectional traffic trunks may exist as well. A traffic trunk is considered bidirectional if the LSPs used to create the traffic trunk include the same ingress and egress LSRs (obviously, in reversed roles) and are created, maintained, and destroyed together. Bidirectional traffic trunks may be symmetrical or asymmetrical in the sense that they are not required to use the same set of LSRs (in reverse order) as long as they have the same termination points.

RFC 2702 (Awduche et al. 1999) defines actions with respect to traffic trunks, which are shown in Table 7.1. In addition to billing, capacity planning, and related functions, measurement of traffic trunk statistics is important in determining more immediate traffic characteristics and trends for use in optimizing network performance. From a TE perspective, the ability to collect this information is essential.

Traffic Trunk Attributes

The attributes of a traffic trunk are values that can be computed or administratively configured to control the behavior of traffic within the trunk. Attributes suggested by RFC 2702 are defined in Table 7.2.

TABLE 7.2. Traffic Trunk Attributes

Attribute	Description
Traffic parameter	Resource needs—average and peak rates, burst tolerance, etc.
Policing	How policing is done
Priority	Intertrunk relative importance
Preemption	Intertrunk relative urgency
Path Adaptivity Resilience	Selection and maintenance criteria used to route the traffic trunk Responsiveness to optimization impetus Responsiveness to network faults
Resource class affinity	Affinity for assigning specific resources to this traffic trunk

TRAFFIC PARAMETER ATTRIBUTE

Statistical approaches have been defined (see, for example, Chang and Thomas 1995) for determining approximately how much real bandwidth is required to support traffic based on well-understood traffic parameters and the queuing behavior of network equipment. These approaches have been used to determine service admissibility in, for example, ATM virtual circuit establishment. Traffic engineering can turn this around somewhat by using the observed traffic parameters of existing flows to determine the size of traffic trunks needed to carry these flows. Alternatively, the sizing of traffic trunks may be determined from measurements of congestion at various points in the network. An admission control function is then used to select specific flows to apply to each traffic trunk.

POLICING ATTRIBUTE

The policing attribute determines specific activity with respect to out-of-compliance traffic associated with a TE traffic trunk. Possible activities include rate limiting (dropping excess traffic), marking or coloring (associating packets with a Cell Loss Priority, Drop Precedence, or a similar marking), or forwarding without action.

Some type of policing action must occur somewhere in a traffic trunk unless all traffic in the trunk is best-effort traffic (implying that no compliance agreement exists). Otherwise, all traffic is treated the same, regardless of its in-compliance status. However, it is not generally desirable to perform policing at every node in the network. Policing for an LSP is generally done only at the ingress for that LSP.

From a TE perspective, however, policing for a traffic trunk is either done or not done. A traffic trunk may start at some point within a service provider's network or may otherwise have been subject to policing (or traffic shaping) already. In this case, it is necessary to be able to disable policing for the traffic trunk.

PRIORITY ATTRIBUTE

Priority is used to determine the order of setup for TE traffic trunks when more than one traffic trunk is pending (for example, during system initialization or fault recovery). A TE solution may need to recompute paths after each successful traffic trunk establishment, particularly when a traffic trunk consumes resources that affect the path selection process for subsequent traffic trunks. Because available resources are consumed with each traffic trunk established, it is likely that each successive traffic trunk will be more constrained than similar traffic trunks established previously.

Priority should take into account the resources each traffic trunk will consume. This is analogous to the problem of fitting as many rocks into a bottle as possible, given a fixed set of rocks of various sizes. Putting larger rocks in first can be the best strategy for getting the largest volume of rock into the bottle. In the TE case, setting up those traffic trunks that consume the most resources later in the setup process increases the likelihood that trunk establishment will fail, even if all of the existing trunks would have succeeded using a different order.

Priority should also take into account the preemption levels of various traffic trunks. Each traffic trunk that is preempted may need to be reestablished. In this case, the system will take longer to establish the full set of traffic trunks if trunks that will be subsequently preempted are established prior to those that might preempt them. As defined in RFC 2702, this occurs automatically because priority and exemption levels are dependent.

PREEMPTION ATTRIBUTE

Preemption is useful in ensuring that high-priority traffic trunks will be routed using a favorable path and in implementing a prioritized restoration process following a network fault. Preemption is defined in two dimensions: the ability of a traffic trunk to preempt other traffic trunks and the ability of a traffic trunk to be preempted by other traffic trunks.

RFC 2702 defines preemption as binary along these two dimensions. That is, a trunk either can or cannot preempt another trunk, and a trunk either can or cannot be preempted by another trunk. If a trunk being established can preempt other trunks and cannot otherwise be established, it will preempt another trunk (that may be preempted) if that other traffic trunk is of a lower priority. In general, a network element processing the setup in this case will preempt existing LSPs—starting with the LSP having the lowest priority—until either there are sufficient resources to satisfy the requirements of the new LSP setup or there are no remaining lower-priority LSPs. Note that LSPs should not actually be preempted if there will not be sufficient resources to establish the new LSP when all lower-priority LSPs have been preempted.

Many implementations handle preemption using a two-level priority:

- The setup priority value affects the probability that a circuit being established will preempt an established circuit.
- The hold priority value affects the probability that an established circuit will be preempted by a circuit being established.

Because a circuit that has been preempted may be reestablished, it is essential that the holding priority never be lower than the setup priority.

Distinct set up and hold priorities may be useful when it is desirable to set up a low-priority circuit that must have a high-priority survivability if it is successfully established. This might be the case for large numbers of short-duration circuits. It would also be the case if disruption of services is intended to be implemented as a breadth-first search for lower-priority circuits to preempt. It is relatively simple to implement the behavior defined in RFC 2702 by always setting setup and hold priorities to the same value.

PATH ATTRIBUTES

Paths used by traffic trunks may be determined in two general ways: using loose or strict explicit routes. The traffic engineer may select key points to include in the explicit path while leaving the actual path used by the traffic trunk between these points to be determined by the interior routing protocol. This approach deforms existing traffic flows by effectively creating new ingress points for trunk traffic, thus affecting the utilization of network resources along routed paths. Alternatively, the traffic engineer may select each hop to be traversed by a traffic trunk based on a priori knowledge of node and link capacity along a strict path. Each approach has advantages and disadvantages.

The traffic engineer may be either a TE automaton or an operator administratively configuring LSPs for use with traffic trunks. In a generalized TE solution, it is possible for variant traffic engineers to each determine and attempt to establish traffic trunks for the same purpose. For instance, a TE automaton may determine one path while an operator has configured another. In general, it is necessary to provide a means to resolve which path will be used to establish a traffic trunk in this case. Specifically, it should be possible to force the system to accept the traffic trunk configured by the network operator. Ideally, the system will report inconsistencies of this type, especially in the event that the configured path is not feasible (or is suboptimal by some threshold value). Alternatively, the path selected by one method (for example, manual configuration) can be treated as the preferred path and will be used as long as this path is not infeasible or seriously suboptimal.

RFC 2702 defines the behavior of arbitrating between a manually configured path and a dynamically computed path by describing manually configured paths as either mandatory or nonmandatory. A mandatory configured path is used regardless of the computed path.

Path maintenance criteria affect whether or not a traffic trunk will be moved in response to specific changes in network topology. In general, a traffic trunk may be established such that the path will not change unless the current path optimization is exceeded by an alternative path optimization by some threshold. In the event that the threshold is exceeded, however, the LSP for the traffic trunk will be reoptimized. If it is the intent that the LSP not be reoptimized, the threshold value would be effectively infinity. Path maintenance criteria may also include other values, such as a delay value (to avoid transient reoptimization). Adaptivity and resilience are subattributes, or aspects, of the path attribute and are discussed in detail in a subsequent section.

In summary, a path attribute includes the strictness of the explicit route, arbitration (mandatory or nonmandatory in RFC 2702), adaptivity, and resilience.

RESOURCE CLASS AFFINITY ATTRIBUTE

Resource classes are also used to constrain the path selection process. Specific resources are either necessarily included or excluded from the path selection process, depending on the affinity value associated with the specific resource. For example, RFC 2702 suggests an affinity value of 1 for explicit inclusion and 2 for exclusion. Using these values, if a resource is assigned an affinity value of 1, then the path selected must include only network elements having this resource. A *resource,* in this context, may be a certain type of queuing behavior or bounded delay characteristic, or it may be a specific set of network elements. The default for unspecified resource class affinities is that associated resources are not considered in selecting a path.

Resource Attributes

This section describes the resource attributes allocation (or subscription) factor and resource class.

ALLOCATION OR SUBSCRIPTION FACTOR

Because of the statistical nature of the distribution of traffic, it is possible to oversubscribe network resources in an effort to achieve better overall utilization. This is most useful when traffic distributions of multiple sources sharing the same resources do not have coincident peaks and troughs. People who are familiar with overbooking of airline reservations are aware that there is usually some association of a lower grade of service with overbooking of resources. This is likely to be true in networks using oversubscription of network resources as well.

Where a very high degree of traffic delivery assurance is desired, undersubscription of network resources may be used. When this is done, a subscription (or allocation) factor is applied to the bandwidth determination for the applicable traffic trunk.

Because network resources typically do not natively support the concept of oversubscribing and undersubscribing their resources, the traffic engineer applies a subscription/allocation factor prior to establishing the traffic trunk. For example, if oversubscribing by 25% corresponds to an allocation factor of 1.25, the traffic engineer would multiply the bandwidth requirement otherwise determined for the traffic trunk by 1.25 prior to requesting the corresponding LSP setup. Note that this is, in effect, an effort to fine tune an effective-bandwidth calculation[4] as might have been required to determine the bandwidth requirements in the first place.

RESOURCE CLASSES

A *resource class* is a characteristic that may be arbitrarily assigned to a resource. Resources belonging to the same resource class are treated similarly by path selection and other policies. The resource class abstraction can be used to determine the set of policies that apply to this resource irrespective of other factors (such as topological location of the resource). These policies include the following:

- Relative preference of resources for path selection in specific trunks
- Explicit restriction of traffic trunk use of a class of resources
- Implementation of a generalized inclusion or exclusion policy
- Prevention of use of nonlocal resources

Resource classes may also be used simply to identify resources.

Constraint-Based Routing

Constraint-based routing is based on the idea of describing a set of link characteristics that are either desirable or undesirable for a particular route and then trying to find a route that has all desirable characteristics and no undesirable characteristics. Using a combination of the metrics defined for traffic engineering and the capabilities of routers, constraint-based routing can substantially reduce the requirements for operator activity necessary to implement TE.

---

4. *Effective bandwidth* is a theoretical approach to determination of a single bandwidth value based on traffic parameters such as peak and average propagation rates, burst duration, and so forth. This concept first arose as early as 1991 and is referred to in RFC 2702 (Awduche et al. 1999) and discussed in Chang and Thomas (1995) and (by a similar name) in Guerin, Ahmadi, and Naghshineh (1991) and is—in concept—not unlike the calculations that airlines apply in determining how much to overbook flights.

An ingress LSR does constraint-based route computations in order to auto-matically compute explicit routes used for traffic trunks originating at that LSR. For TE, the traffic engineer would initiate this process.

The traffic engineer specifies the ingress and egress of a traffic trunk and assigns a set of characteristics for a desirable route. These characteristics define constraints in terms of performance needs and other aspects. Constraint-based routing then finds an explicit route that will satisfy these constraints among the set of available routes. Note that selecting an optimal route requires determining all possible routes for N + 1 TE trunks (assuming *N* existing TE trunks) and selecting the optimal set of routes in reestablishing the full set of TE trunks plus the new one requested. This is a task that is eas-ily recognizable as NP-complete.

An example of use of constraint-based routing to satisfy a traffic engineer-ing need is the attempt to move a portion of the traffic on a congested link to another link. Assigning the congested link to a resource class that would be treated as an undesirable characteristic of the desired route is a simple and direct way to represent the desired constraint. The traffic engineer defines a portion of the traffic that would normally traverse the congested link (possibly in terms of a set of destination addresses) and initiates the constraint-based routing process. The traffic engineer causes a set of ingress LSRs to each seek a new path that satisfies the constraint that it not use any link that is in the resource class associated with the undesirable (congested) link.

Although finding the optimal route using constraint-based routing is known to be computationally difficult for almost any realistic constraint-limited routing problem, a simple heuristic can be used to find a route satisfying a set of constraints—if one exists. The traffic engineer may simply prune resources that do not match the traffic trunk attributes and run a shortest-path route computation on the residual graph. Other approaches may be used as well.

Continuing the previous example, ingress LSRs prune the set of available links known to them (for example, as a result of using a link-state routing protocol) of all links belonging to the resource class of the congested link (possibly a "congested" resource class is defined for all such links). These ingress LSRs can then run a route computation (using the pruned link-state information) and establish explicit routes on the basis of their results. The ingress LSRs then use this explicit route solely for routing the portion of traffic defined. Because the ingress LSRs no longer route this traffic via the congested link, the congestion on that link would be reduced by an amount that may be as much as the amount of traffic associated with that defined portion of the traffic now being forwarded on the new explicit route.

These procedures, being heuristic in nature, will not necessarily find the optimal solution. In addition, successive applications of these approaches may lead to failure to find a route for one or more traffic trunks when all such traffic trunks could have been accommodated with an optimal solution. This implies that it will be necessary to tear down TE trunks at some point to avoid increasingly suboptimal constraint-based route determinations.

To perform the automated constraint-based routing computation in the example, the information provided by the link-state routing protocol must include information about the links that would allow ingress LSRs to determine what links satisfy which constraints. For example, when the congested link was assigned to a resource class, this assignment would have to be advertised in the link-state routing protocol in common use by LSRs in the TE domain.

Support for constraint-based routing computations is currently being developed in the IGP routing protocols IS-IS (Intelligent Scheduling and Information System) and OSPF (Open Shortest Path First).

Path Establishment and Maintenance

The path used by a traffic trunk may be determined automatically by using traffic trunk attributes to either explicitly include or exclude network resources and then performing a path computation. This is referred to as *constraint-based routing* in RFC 2702 (Awduche et al. 1999). Once a path is determined, the path is established and maintained using the adaptivity and resiliency aspects of the path attribute as in the following subsections.

USE OF STRICTNESS OF THE EXPLICIT ROUTE

The traffic engineer computes an explicit route for use in establishing the traffic trunk. If strict explicit routing of the traffic trunk is not required, the traffic engineer can perform this task in the absence of perfect knowledge of the network. If strict routing is required, determination of the entire strict route is part of the computation process. If the traffic engineer starts with imperfect knowledge of the network topology, the LSP signaling process may be used as an aid in computing the explicit path. For example, the Record Route object may be used in RSVP-TE signaling for explicit route setup. Signaling of the explicit route is accomplished using either CR-LDP or RSVP-TE and including the Explicit Route object.

USE OF THE ADAPTIVITY ASPECT OF THE PATH ATTRIBUTE

Path reoptimization is controlled by the adaptivity subattribute of the path control and maintenance attributes. This aspect determines whether or not the LSP associated with a traffic trunk will be reoptimized as a result of changes to network resources. Control of this behavior is highly desirable because reoptimization itself is not always desirable. To understand why this is so, consider that there must be some reason why a new path is considered to be more optimal. Maybe there are more resources, or less congestion, associated with a new path. Consequently, it is reasonable to expect that packets may be delivered more quickly along the new path; however, this can cause trouble for specific applications that are sensitive to either delay variation or to ordering of packet delivery. For these applications, reoptimization is undesirable.

Adaptivity is preventable in signaling if (in CR-LDP, for example) it is possible to pin a route explicitly. An explicit route may also be pinned by being strictly routed at all hops. As described in the Piggyback Label Distribution Using RSVP section in Chapter 6, it is possible to use the Record Route object to determine the exact route currently being used by an LSP and then use this information to pin the LSP. Maintenance of a pinned explicit route is simpler because it is unnecessary to retain information required to reroute the LSP at every network element that might otherwise be required to do so.

USE OF THE RESILIENCE ASPECT OF THE PATH ATTRIBUTE

Reoptimization is distinct from resilience. A traffic trunk that is not subject to reoptimization can be required to be resilient to link and node failures along its established path. Resiliency is implicit for LSPs that are adaptive to reoptimization.

The resilience aspect can be broken into two parts: basic and extended resiliency. Basic resiliency determines whether a traffic trunk is subject to automatic rerouting as a result of a partial path failure (one or more segments fail). Extended resiliency determines the specific actions taken in response to a fault—for example, the order in which specified alternative paths are considered. Support for resilient behavior depends on interactions with underlying routing technology, both in detecting a fault and in selecting a new path.

Resilience at the local level is only possible if the original path was a loosely specified portion of an explicit route or if the fault is part of a segment where there is more than one strictly specified explicit route provided for this purpose.

Load Distribution Using TE Traffic Trunks

Being able to distribute traffic across multiple similar-cost LSPs between an ingress and egress pair is an important TE capability. For example, the aggregate traffic between the two nodes may be more than can be supported using any single path between the two nodes. Distributing the traffic as multiple substreams allows the system to provide forwarding that exceeds the limitations of single links in paths between the two nodes.

This distribution can be done using MPLS by establishing multiple LSPs (effectively as a single combined traffic trunk), each of which will carry a portion of the traffic for the combined traffic. To do this, however, the ingress LSR must be capable of assigning packets to each of the multiple LSPs in an intelligent fashion.

For example, assume two LSPs are established to carry the traffic from an ingress LSR to an egress LSR for the same aggregate traffic. One is expected to carry two-thirds of the traffic, whereas the other carries one-third. In this scenario, the ingress LSR must map corresponding portions of the incoming traffic aggregate to each LSP. It is desirable that this mapping be done in such a way as to ensure that packets that are part of the same source-destination flow follow the same LSP as a safeguard against out-of-order delivery.

Fault Handling

In general, four functions are associated with fault handling:

- Detection
- Isolation
- Notification
- Restoration

These functions are not necessarily performed in the order listed. For example, notification may need to occur before isolation can begin, and restoration may have begun before a fault was detected (for example, establishing a redundant circuit in anticipation of failure) and may in any case begin before notification takes place. In some technologies (for exampe, IP routing), detection and isolation are not separable functions.

Because TE uses explicitly routed LSPs, mechanisms intrinsic to the underlying routing infrastructure will not necessarily be sufficient for recovering from a fault, particularly in strictly routed (or pinned) portions of the LSP. Because (by default) routing is blind to the paths taken by an explicitly routed LSP, MPLS needs to provide separate mechanisms for detecting a fault in an LSP, notifying the ingress (especially if the fault is not locally repairable), and initiating restoration of service.

Because it is possible that MPLS is using technology that may provide some alternative fault recovery mechanisms, fault recovery mechanisms defined specifically for MPLS must be able to be disabled.

Fault recovery must also take into account the priority and precedence attributes of the traffic trunk.

Approaches

This section describes signaling approaches for support of traffic engineering.

LDP

LDP may be used in a simple TE application in which a TE traffic trunk is desirable from one LSR to another, and a degenerate explicit route (in which only the egress is specified) is sufficient to satisfy TE requirements.

In this case, the two LSRs may be assumed not to be directly connected, and an LSP tunnel is constructed between them. The specific mechanism used to accomplish this is that the ingress LSR establishes an LSP associated with an address prefix FEC and that matches the prefix length of an address of the egress LSR. The ingress LSR now maps traffic onto this LSP using the specific FEC defined for the corresponding traffic trunk.

This process may be extended to include additional LSPs in tandem. In this case, either the egress LSR is also the ingress to one or more further LSPs, the ingress LSR is egress to one or more LSPs, or both LSRs are both ingress and egress to LSPs. The LSPs in this discussion are LSPs for which there is a similar mapping of TE forwarding classes corresponding to a traffic trunk that uses two or more LSPs in tandem.

Because it is not possible to pin an LSP routed from an ingress to an egress LSR using LDP alone, a traffic trunk established using this approach is both adaptive and resilient by nature. Therefore, this approach cannot be used to establish traffic trunks for which either of these properties is undesirable.

In addition, it is not possible to explicitly assign resources from the path used for this approach via the LDP signaling protocol. If it is necessary to assign resources to a traffic trunk explicitly via the signaling protocol, some other approach must be used.

CR-LDP EXPLICIT ROUTES

The difference between LDP and CR-LDP is that CR-LDP supports explicit routes and allocation of resources. CR-LDP support of TE traffic trunks is thus very similar to that provided by LDP, but without the restrictions that apply when LDP is used by itself.

Because CR-LDP has the Explicit Route object (and procedures to support its use), a traffic trunk LSP can be fully specified as a set of strict explicit hops. CR-LDP supports explicit pinning of an explicit route as well. CR-LDP also includes extensions to provide RSVP-like resource allocation in setting up explicitly routed LSPs.

RSVP TUNNELS

RSVP-TE (Awduche et al. w.i.p.) defines procedures for use in establishing explicitly routed LSPs using standard RSVP messages with extensions.

Extensions to the base RSVP protocol are defined as objects. These objects are opaque to RSVP speakers that are not MPLS enabled; however, support for piggyback label distribution using RSVP requires all participants to be MPLS enabled.

An explicit-route LSP is constructed using procedures defined in RSVP-TE and including an Explicit Route object in a Path message. Support for route pinning is provided by including the Record Route object in both Path and Resv messages and then including the Explicit Route object with a fully specified strict explicit route in all subsequent Path messages.

7.4 Virtual Private Networks

In general, the distinction between a virtual private network (VPN) and an actual private network (APN) is that in the VPN case, network resources are shared among multiple VPN instances while maintaining the notion of privacy between VPN instances. In an APN, privacy is a result of not sharing network resources with other private networks.

To effectively provide the illusion of a private network using shared resources, it is necessary to support private address spaces and to provide for separation of traffic by preventing leakage of traffic from one VPN to either another VPN or to the Internet and by providing some level of isolation of VPN traffic from the effects of traffic in other networks sharing the same resources.

Methods of isolating traffic from sharing effects (among VPN alternatives discussed to date) fall into one of four categories:

- No isolation (best effort)
- Relative levels of service (copper, gold, and platinum)
- Committed Data Rate (CDR)
- CDR+ (at least CDR)

Approaches

Numerous proposals for supporting VPNs using MPLS have been discussed within the MPLS working group. The section entitled Virtual Private Networks,

Traffic Engineering, and Optimized Multipathing Draft Development in Chapter 2 provides a brief overview of specific drafts on the subject.

No single approach has become a standard; however, there are two major contenders: VPNs using BGP and MPLS, and explicitly routed VPNs. It is most likely at present that BGP-MPLS VPNs will emerge as the commonly used approach, in part because it is the approach advocated by the current market leader.

BGP-MPLS VPNS

RFC 2547 (Rosen and Rekhter 1999) is an informational RFC that describes how BGP and MPLS would be used to provide a VPN service. Unfortunately, this procedure is dependent on BGP-MPLS (Rekhter and Rosen 2000), which is not yet completely defined.

The essence of the procedure is that BGP is used to propagate VPN-specific routes to populate separate forwarding tables in the VPN service provider's network. RFC 2547 defines a provider edge (PE) router that must determine which forwarding table to use based on which customer edge (CE) router it was received from.

Some measure of scalability is achieved in this approach by limiting the distribution of VPN-specific routes to those PE routers that attach CE routers within the given VPN. In this way, each PE router only needs to maintain routes for CE routers to which it is directly attached.

Route distribution for VPN support using BGP is accomplished using BGP multiprotocol extensions (defined in RFC 2283 [Bates et al. 1998]) and a new Address Family Identifier (AFI) and Subsequent Address Family Identifier (SAFI)—1 and 128, respectively—that identify the VPN-IPv4 address family. Addresses from this address family are 12 bytes long and include an 8-byte route distinguisher (RD) and an IPv4 address (prefix). The mapping between RDs and specific VPNs is not guaranteed because an RD need only be unique to the PE set participating in a VPN and will vary across service provider domains. A PE determines which routes to distribute for a given VPN based on target VPN attributes that are associated with per-site VPN-specific forwarding tables. Association of target VPN attributes with specific sites is determined by configuration.

BGP-MPLS VPN routes are distributed using peer-to-peer BGP direct connections or connections via a route reflector. The BGP Update messages used to distribute these routes include MPLS labels corresponding to each route (using appropriate AFI/SAFI and address length values). Procedures and formats for carrying labels in a BGP Update message are defined in Rekhter and Rosen (w.i.p.) and described in Piggyback Label Distribution Using BGP, in Chapter 6.

Setup and maintenance of an LSP between two PE routers that are not directly connected is accomplished using LDP, CR-LDP, or RSVP-TE, with or without explicit routes.

EXPLICITLY ROUTED VPNS

Several approaches exist and have been proposed for supporting a VPN service using explicitly routed LSPs. This approach is essentially similar to creation of multiple instances of TE traffic trunk overlays.

Although most proposals are currently either entirely proprietary or based on proprietary extensions to a TE-based solution, there are several common distinctions between this general approach and BGP-MPLS VPNs. Some of the ways in which explicitly routed VPNs may differ from BGP-MPLS VPNs include the following:

- Standard VPN identifiers—as defined in RFC 2685 (Fox and Gleeson 1999)—may be used instead of route distinguishers.
- Labels may be consistently distributed using a single signaling protocol, such as RSVP-TE or CR-LDP.
- BGP peering with CE routers is not required.
- Customer equipment need not have any routing capability.
- VPN support may be provided independent of the network layer in use by the VPN user.

References

Awduche, Daniel O., Lou Berger, Der-Hwa Gan, Tony Li, Vijay Srinivasan, and George Swallow. RSVP-TE: Extensions to RSVP for LSP tunnels; a work in progress.

Awduche, Daniel O., Joe Malcolm, Johnson Agogbua, Mike O'Dell, and Jim McManus. 1999 (September). Requirements for traffic engineering over MPLS. RFC 2702. Available at http://www.isi.edu/in-notes/rfc2702.txt.

Bates, Tony, Ravi Chandra, Dave Katz, and Yakov Rekhter. 1998 (February). Multiprotocol extensions for BGP-4. RFC 2283. Available at http://www.isi.edu/in-notes/rfc2283.txt.

Chang, C. S., and J. A. Thomas. 1995. Effective bandwidth in high-speed networks. *IEEE Journal of Selected Areas in Communication* 13(6):1091–1100.

Fox, Barbara A., and Bryan Gleeson. 1999 (September). Virtual private networks identifier. RFC 2685. Available at http://www.isi.edu/in-notes/rfc2685.txt.

Gleeson, Bryan, Arthur Lin, Juha Heinanen, Grenville Armitage, and Andrew Malis. 2000 (February). A framework for IP based virtual private networks. RFC 2764. Available at http://www.isi.edu/in-notes/rfc2764.txt.

Guerin, R., H. Ahmadi, and M. Naghshineh. 1991. Equivalent capacity and its application to bandwidth allocation in high-speed networks. *IEEE Journal of Selected Areas in Communication* 9(7):968–981.

Jamoussi, Bilel, ed. Constraint-based LSP setup using LDP; a work in progress. http://www.ietf.org/internet-drafts/draft-ietf-mpls-cr-ldp-04.txt.

Le Faucheur, Francois, Liwen Wu, Bruce Davie, Shahram Davari, Pasi Vaananen, Ram Krishnan, Pierrick Cheval, and Juha Heinanen. MPLS support of Differentiated Services; a work in progress.

Rekhter, Yakov, and Eric C. Rosen. 2000 (January). Carrying label information in BGP-4, version 4. Internet Draft (draft-ietf-mpls-bgp4-mpls-04). Available at http://www.ietf.org/internet-drafts/draft-ietf-mpls-bgp4-mpls-04.txt.

Rosen, Eric C., and Yakov Rekhter. 1999 (March). BGP/MPLS VPNs. RFC 2547. Available at http://www.isi.edu/in-notes/rfc2547.txt.

GLOSSARY

ACRONYM EXPANSIONS

AAL	ATM Adaptation Layer
AF	Assured Forwarding
AFI	Address Family Identifier
APN	actual private network
ARIS	Aggregate Route-based IP Switching
ARP	Address Resolution Protocol
AS	Autonomous System
ATM	Asynchronous Transfer Mode
BA	Behavior Aggregate
BGP	Border Gateway Protocol
BOF	Birds of a Feather
CAC	Call (or Connection) Admission Control
CE	customer edge (or customer equipment)
CLIP	Classical IP and ARP over ATM
CLP	Cell Loss Priority
CPCS	Common Part Convergence Sublayer
CPE	customer premises (or provided) equipment
CR-LDP	Constraint-based Routing Label Distribution Protocol
CSR	cell switching router
DE	Discard Eligibility
DLCI	Data Link Connection Identifier
DLL	data link layer (L2)
DoD	downstream on-demand label distribution (mode)
DSCP	Differentiated Services Code (Control) Point
DU	downstream unsolicited label distribution (mode)
ECN	Explicit Congestion Notification

EF	Expedited Forwarding
EGP	exterior gateway protocol
E-LSP	EXP-inferred-PSC LSP
EXP	Experimental bits
FANP	Flow Attribute Notification Protocol
FEC	forwarding equivalence class
FF	Fixed Filter
FIB	forwarding information base
FR	Frame Relay
FTN	FEC-to-NHLFE map
GSMP	General (or Generic) Switch Management Protocol
ICMP	Internet Control Message Protocol
IEEE	Institute of Electrical and Electronics Engineers
IETF	Internet Engineering Task Force
IFMP	Ipsilon's Flow Management Protocol
IGP	interior gateway protocol
ILM	Incoming Label Map
ION	Internetworking over NBMA
IP	Internet Protocol
I-PNNI	Integrated PNNI
IPv4	IP version 4
IPv6	IP version 6
ISP	Internet service provider
LAN	local area network
LANE	LAN emulation
LC-ATM	label switching controlled—ATM
LC-FR	label switching controlled—Frame Relay
LDP	Label Distribution Protocol[1]
LER	label edge router
LIS	logical IP subnet
L-LSP	Label-only-inferred-PSC LSP
LSP	label-switched path

---

1. By convention, the term *label distribution protocol* refers specifically to the protocol defined in MPLS only when capitalized. Otherwise, it refers to the general category of protocols that may also distribute labels.

LSR	label switching (switched or switch) router
MIB	Management Information Base
MPLS	Multiprotocol Label Switching
MPOA	Multi-Protocol over ATM
NBMA	nonbroadcast multiple access (networks)
NHLFE	Next Hop Label Forwarding Entry
NHRP	Next Hop Resolution Protocol
NHS	Next Hop Server
NLRI	network layer reachability information
OA	Ordered Aggregate
OSI	Open Systems Interconnection
OSPF	Open Shortest Path First
PAR	PNNI augmented routing
PDU	protocol data unit
PE	provider edge
PHB	per-hop behavior
PHP	penultimate hop pop
PNNI	Private Network-to-Network Interface
POS	Packet over (on) SONET
PPP	Point-to-Point Protocol
PSC	PHB scheduling class
PSTN	Public Switched Telephone (Telephony) Network
PVC	permanent virtual circuit
QoS	quality of service
RD	route distinguisher
RFC	Request for Comments
ROLC	Routing Over Large Clouds
RSVP	Reservation Protocol
SAFI	Subsequent Address Family Identifier
SE	Shared Explicit
SITA	Switching IP Through ATM
SNPA	Subnetwork Points of Attachment
SONET	Synchronous Optical Network
STII	Internet Stream Protocol version II
SVC	switched virtual circuit

TDP	Tag Distribution Protocol
TE	traffic engineering
TLV	type-length-value
TM	traffic management
TTL	Time to Live
VC	virtual circuit
VCI or VCID	virtual circuit identifier
VP	virtual path
VPCI	virtual path and circuit identifier
VPI	virtual path identifier
VPN	virtual private network

DEFINITIONS

abstract node   An abstraction used in describing an explicit route. An abstract node may be a network element, a group of network elements sharing an address prefix, or an Autonomous System. An abstract node consisting of exactly one network element is called a *simple abstract node*.

actual private network   A term invented for comparison with virtual private network (VPN).

adjacent   Having a direct logical link. Either directly connected physically, or connected using an approach that makes intervening devices transparent in a logical context—for example, tunneling.

aggregation   Grouping or bundling traffic requiring similar forwarding. Distinct from merging, generally, because it may be desirable to separate aggregate traffic at some point without having to resort to a routing decision at L3 for all packets within the aggregate.

Assured Forwarding   A per-hop behavior (PHB) defined for Differentiated Services that provides for four classes of PHB, each having three levels of drop precedence. Assured Forwarding also requires that packets within a class not be reordered, regardless of the drop precedence. Assured Forwarding does not define a quantifiable value for delay or delay variation of packets forwarded.

Autonomous System   In interdomain routing, an administrative domain identified with an AS number.

Behavior Aggregate   IP packets that require the same Differentiated Services behavior at the point where they are crossing a link.

Border Gateway Protocol   The only exterior gateway routing protocol. Currently version 4 is in use. A routing protocol used in routing between administrative domains.

bridge   A device used to forward frames at the data-link layer.

Cell Loss Priority   A bit in the AAL5 ATM header indicating that the cell can be dropped earlier under congested conditions.

Connection (or Call) Admission Control   Use of some approach to determine whether or not a requested service requirement can reasonably expect to be met by a device, prior to committing to provide the requested service at the device.

conservative retention mode   Labels are requested and retained only when needed for a specific next hop. Unnecessary labels are immediately released.

content addressable memory   A memory device that allows a key to be compared to the contents of all memory locations at the same time. Content addressable memory is roughly a hardware analogue of a software hashing algorithm.

control word   An instruction, index, or key into a table of instructions, generally at the (virtual) machine level.

Data Link Connection Identifier   Used in Frame Relay to identify a circuit connection between adjacent Frame Relay switches.

data link layer   Layer 2 of the OSI model; the layer between the physical and network layers.

Differentiated Services (DiffServ)   An IETF standard for providing different classes of service based on some common sets of assumptions about queuing behavior on a hop-by-hop basis. Because the basis for specific treatment is explicitly carried in packets, rather than requiring local storage of packet classification information, this approach to providing quality of service (QoS) is often referred to as "less state-full" than, for example, the Integrated Services QoS model.

Discard Eligibility   A bit in the Frame Relay header indicating that the frame can be discarded under congested conditions.

domain of (label) significance   The portion of a network consisting of logically connected logical interfaces with a common knowledge of the significance (meaning) of a label. A label only has meaning upon arrival at a logical interface if that interface was represented in the process during which the meaning was originally negotiated.

downstream   In the direction of expected traffic flow. Applies to traffic that is part of a specific forwarding equivalence class.

downstream label allocation   Label negotiation in which the downstream LSR determines what label will be used. This is the only currently supported approach.

downstream on-demand label distribution mode   Labels are allocated and provided to the upstream peer only when requested. This mode is most useful when the upstream LSR is using conservative label retention or is not merge capable (or, as is likely, both).

downstream unsolicited label distribution mode   Labels are allocated and provided to the upstream peer at any time (typically in conjunction with advertisement of a new route). Most useful when the upstream neighbor is using liberal retention mode.

egress   Point of exit from an MPLS context or domain. The egress of an LSP is the logical point at which the determination to pop a label associated with an LSP is made. The label may actually be popped at the LSR making this determination or at the one prior to it (in the penultimate hop pop case). Egress from MPLS in general is the point at which the last label is removed (resulting in removal of the label stack).

Expedited Forwarding   A per-hop behavior defined for Differentiated Services that requires a network node to provide a well-defined minimum departure rate service for a configurable departure rate such that if incoming traffic is conditioned not to exceed this minimum departure rate, packets are effectively not queued within the node. Expedited Forwarding ensures that, for conditioned traffic, the delay at any node is bounded and quantifiable.

explicit route   A route specified as a nonempty list of hops that must be part of the route used. If an explicit route is strict, only specified hops may be used. If an explicit route is loose, all specified hops must be included, in order, in the resulting path, but the path is otherwise unrestricted.

extranet   From the perspective of a private network, any other network, including all other networks.

filtering database   Used in some bridging technologies to determine what interfaces an L2 frame will not be forwarded on.

Fixed Filter   A reservation style that is useful in establishing a point-to-point LSP from one ingress to one egress LSR.

flooding   The process of forwarding data on all, or most, interfaces in order to ensure that the receiver gets at least one copy.

forwarding database   Information used to make a forwarding determination.

forwarding determination   The process used to determine the interface to be used to forward data. This process may or may not be directly driven by a route determination.

forwarding equivalence class   A description of the criteria used to determine that a set of packets is to be forwarded in an equivalent fashion (along the same logical LSP). Forwarding equivalence classes are defined in the base LDP specification and may be extended through the use of additional parameters (such as is the case with CR-LDP). FECs are also represented in other label distribution protocols.

frame   A message encapsulation generally consisting of a DLL header, a payload—frequently consisting of at least part of a network-layer packet—and (possibly) a trailer. Normally encapsulated by physical-layer framing.

FTN   FEC-to-NHLFE map, used to insert unlabeled packets onto an LSP.

hard state   State information that remains valid until explicitly invalidated.

implicit null label   A label value given to an upstream neighbor when it is desirable to have that LSR pop one label prior to forwarding the packet. This behavior is commonly referred to as penulitimate hop pop (PHP).

Incoming Label Map   Used to find the NHLFE for determining forwarding information for a labeled packet.

independent control mode   Mode in which an LSR allocates and provides labels to upstream peers at any time. This mode may be used, for instance, when routing is used to drive label distribution and it is desirable to supply applicable labels to routing peers at about the same time as new routes are advertised.

ingress   Point at which an MPLS context or domain is entered. The ingress of an LSP is the point at which a label is pushed onto the label stack (possibly resulting in the creation of the label stack).

Integrated Services (IntServ)   An IETF quality-of-service standard. In essence, QoS is assured based on signaling end-to-end service requirements using a common signaling protocol. (RSVP is the only common end-to-end protocol currently defined for this purpose.) These service requirements are then mapped to specific queuing parameters for each specific medium type that may be present in such an end-to-end service. The use of CAC and traffic disciplining techniques allows this approach to effectively guarantee a requested service requirement. Because packets are classified to determine what level of service they require, and the classification information must be retained at each node, this QoS approach is often referred to as the "state-full" QoS model.

interdomain routing   Routing between administrative domains. Supported currently by BGP version 4.

interface   Physical or logical end point of a link between devices.

Internet service provider (ISP)   Provider of an access service to the Internet, usually for a charge. Access service charges may be flat rate or based on either rate or usage. Service providers make up the Internet through complex tiering and peering relationships.

intranet   A private network.

L1, L2, L3   physical, data link, and network layers (respectively).

label   A fixed-size field contained in a message header that may be used as an exact-match key in determining how to forward a protocol data unit.

label distribution   Process by which labels are negotiated between peer LSRs.

label edge router   A term often used to indicate an LSR that is able to provide ingress to and egress from an LSP. In individual implementations, this tends to be a function of the capabilities of device interfaces more than of the overall device. In theory, it is possible for a device to be an LER and not an LSR (if it is not able to swap labels, for instance); however, it is unlikely that such an LER would be generally useful or make any particular sense in a cost-benefit analysis.

label stack   Successive labels in an MPLS shim header in order from the top to the bottom of the stack.

label swapping   Replacing an input label with a corresponding output label.

label-switched path   Path along which labeled packets are forwarded. Packets forwarded using any label are forwarded along the same path as other packets using the same label.

label switching   Switching based on use of labels.

label switching router   A device that participates in one or more routing protocols and uses the route information derived from routing protocol exchanges to drive LSP setup and maintenance. Such a device typically distributes labels to peers and uses these labels (when provided as part of data presented for forwarding) to forward label-encapsulated L3 packets. In general, an LSR may or may not be able to forward non-label-encapsulated data and provide ingress/egress to LSPs (that is, to perform what is frequently referred to as the label edge router, or LER, function).

liberal retention mode   Labels are retained whenever received. This mode is useful when the ability to change quickly to a new LSP is desirable; however, it may result in unacceptable memory consumption for LSRs with many interfaces.

link   Physical or logical connection between two end points.

logical interface   An interface associated with a specific encapsulation. Data arriving at the corresponding physical (or lower-level logical) interface that is encapsulated for a specific logical interface is de-encapsulated and delivered to that logical interface.

merging   A key function in making MPLS scalable in the number of labels consumed at each LSR. Merging is the process by which packets from multiple sources are typically delivered to a single destination or destination prefix. It is distinct from aggregation in that (in most cases) the decision to merge traffic implies that the possibility of being required to separate the merged traffic at a later point is not significant at the point where merging is being done.

network layer   Layer 3 of the OSI model; the layer between the data-link and transport layers. Normally encapsulated in one or more data-link layer frames.

Next Hop Label Forwarding Information Entry   Contains all of the information needed to forward a labeled packet to the next hop. This information includes push, pop, or swap instructions; the new label (or labels in the event that multiple pushes are called for); the output interface; and other information that may be needed to forward the packet to the next hop.

Ordered Aggregate   The set of Behavior Aggregates that share an ordering constraint. For example, a set of PHB values that can be ordered relative to one another, such as AF drop precedences within an AF class.

ordered control mode   Mode in which an LSR only allocates and provides labels to an upstream peer when it is either the egress for the resulting LSP or it has received a label from downstream for the resulting LSP.

packet   A message encapsulation consisting of a network-layer header and payload.

packet switching   An approach used to forward L3 packets from an input L3 logical interface to an output L3 logical interface that may reasonably be optimized for hardware switching—similar to switching at the data-link layer.

penultimate hop pop   A process by which the peer immediately upstream of the egress LSR is asked to pop a label prior to forwarding the packet to the egress LSR. Using LDP, this is done by assigning the special value of the implicit Null label. This allows the egress to push the work of popping the label to its upstream neighbor, possibly allowing for a more optimal processing of the remaining packet. Note that this can be done because once the label has been used to determine the next-hop information for the last hop, the label is no longer useful. Using PHP is helpful because it allows the packet to be treated as an unlabeled packet by the last hop. Using PHP, it is possible to implement an "LSR" that never uses labels.

per-hop behavior   A Differentiated Services behavioral definition. A PHB is defined at a node by the combination of a Differentiated Services Code Point (DSCP) and a set of configured behaviors.

PHB scheduling class   The nonempty set of per-hop behaviors that apply to the Behavior Aggregates belonging to a given Ordered Aggregate.

piggyback   Intuitive term for the use of routing, or routing-related, protocols to carry labels.

pop   In a label-switching context, the process of removing the top-level label (the label at the head of the label stack) from the label stack.

protocol data unit   A unit of data used in specific protocol interactions. It may be generically described as a format for encapsulation and forwarding of protocol messages between protocol entities. Messages may span multiple PDUs, a single PDU may contain multiple messages, and PDUs may be nested.

push   In a label-switching context, the process of adding a new top-level label (which becomes the new label at the head of the label stack) to the label stack.

quality of service   Specific handling or treatment of packets, often in an end-to-end service. Best-effort (also sometimes referred to as "worst-effort") is currently the lowest level of packet treatment, other than an "unconditional drop" service. Currently, there are two models for providing QoS in an IP network: Integrated Services (IntServ) and Differentiated Services (DiffServ).

route computation   The process by which routers compute entries for a route table. Route table entries are subsequently used in route determination.

route determination   The process of selecting a route based on header information in packets and route table entries established previously via route computation. Typically, a route is determined using the longest match of the network-layer destination address in L3 packets against a network address prefix in the route table.

router   A device used to forward packets at the network (L3) layer.

routing   A scheme for selecting one of many possible paths.

scalability   A reflection of the way in which system complexity grows as a function of some system parameter, such as size. If growth in system complexity is approximately linear with respect to growth in system size, for instance, the size scalability of the system is generally considered to be good.

Shared Explicit   Reservation style in which path resources are explicitly shared among multiple senders and receivers. Useful when it is desirable to increase reservation resources or establish a new reservation without double-booking resources.

shim header   An encoding of the MPLS label stack. Present for all media when a label stack is in use. (The presence of the label stack is indicated either by protocol numbers or connection identifiers in the L2 encapsulation.)

slow-path forwarding   Used to refer to processing of exception packets in which the packet is handled via direct intervention of a system CPU resource that is not normally used in fast-path (optimized) forwarding.

soft state   State information that becomes out of date if not refreshed.

source route   An explicit route specified from the source toward the destination.

switching   Ushering input data or messages more or less directly to an output; typically based on a simplistic recognition mechanism (such as an exact match of a fixed-length field).

traffic engineer   An operator or automaton with the express purpose of minimizing congestion in a network. Traffic engineering is an application of a traffic engineer.

traffic engineering   An application of constraint-based routing in which a traffic engineer uses a set of link characteristics to select a route and assigns specific traffic to that route.

type-length-value   An object description with highly intuitive meaning; that is, the object consists of three fields: type, length, and value. Type gives the semantic meaning of the value, length gives the number of bytes in the value field (which may be fixed by the type), and value consists of *length* bytes of data in a format consistent with *type*. This object format is used in LDP and several other protocols.

upstream   Direction from which traffic is expected to arrive. Applies to a specific forwarding equivalence class.

upstream label allocation   A scheme by which the upstream peer is allowed to select the label that will be used in forwarding labeled traffic for a specific forwarding equivalence class. Not currently supported in MPLS.

virtual X   Pseudo-*X*. Not quite or really an *X*. A small white lie.

INDEX

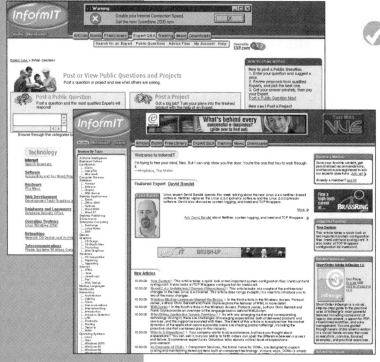

Register Your Book

at www.aw.com/cseng/register

You may be eligible to receive:

- Advance notice of forthcoming editions of the book
- Related book recommendations
- Chapter excerpts and supplements of forthcoming titles
- Information about special contests and promotions throughout the year
- Notices and reminders about author appearances, tradeshows, and online chats with special guests

Contact us

If you are interested in writing a book or reviewing manuscripts prior to publication, please write to us at:

Editorial Department
Addison-Wesley Professional
75 Arlington Street, Suite 300
Boston, MA 02116 USA
Email: AWPro@aw.com

Addison-Wesley

Visit us on the Web: http://www.aw.com/cseng